Vocabulary for GCSE Spanish

Geoff Taylor

MARY GLASGOW PUBLICATIONS

We are grateful to the following for allowing us to reproduce published material: ABC, Banco de Bilbao, Consorcio regional de transportes de Madrid, El Corte Inglés, El Olivio Bar, Glaxo, Oficina de información y turismo Pamplona, Pizza-Pizza, Ya

Every effort has been made to trace the copyright holders but the publishers will be pleased to make the necessary arrangements at the first opportunity if there are any omissions.

The author would like to thank the following for their assistance: Isabel Melero Orta (Pamplona), Ana Saborido Rey (Madrid), John Connor (Cheltenham), Barrie Mordue (for typing the manuscript).

Designed by Ennismore Design, London

First published in 1996 by
Mary Glasgow Publications
an imprint of Stanley Thornes (Publishers) Ltd
Ellenborough House
Wellington Street
Cheltenham
GLOS GL50 1YW

99 00 01 02 / 10 9 8 7 6 5 4 3

A catalogue record for this book is available from the British Library.

ISBN 0–7487–2852–X

Printed and bound in Great Britain by Redwood Books, Trowbridge, Wiltshire

Contents

Introduction

◆ Aims

The aim of this book is to provide you with the vocabulary you need in the early years of learning Spanish – particularly at key stage 4 (years 10 and 11) for GCSE. It is based on the syllabuses of the major GCSE exam boards and gives most of the words you need for **Foundation Tier**, although you can expect to come across some unfamiliar words as well. For **Higher Tier**, examples are given for the sort of words you may encounter, and there is also space for you to add examples of your own as you meet them – the responsibility lies with you.

◆ How the book is arranged

The vocabulary topics are arranged in groups relating to the five areas of experience as laid out in the National Curriculum. There is also a general section with words that you can use for many topics. Each topic is divided into sub-sections with the vocabulary grouped in small sections to make it easier to learn. Each topic contains examples of useful phrases, and there are also activities and puzzles spread throughout the book to give further practice. At the back of the book, you will find sections to help you with your GCSE work: Building up Vocabulary, Words to Watch Out For, Writing Tips and Dictionary Skills.

◆ How do I learn vocabulary?

1   The learning of vocabulary (like the learning of grammar) is absolutely essential if you are going to make any real progress in Spanish.

2   Try to set yourself realistic targets – say you will learn so many new words every week, or day.

3   Get someone else (a member of your family or a friend) to test you.

4   Make learning cards to help you remember those words that are causing problems.

5   If you have a computer, you could devise a simple program to reinforce the vocabulary.

There is no doubt that as your vocabulary increases, so too will your confidence. You will become increasingly better equipped to tackle work in all skill areas of the language, whether in class, for homework or in exams. Of course, if you have a good working vocabulary, any visit you make to a Spanish-speaking country will be that much more enjoyable.

General

◆ Colours

los colores	colour
blanco	white
negro	black
gris	grey
rojo	red
amarillo	yellow
verde	green
azul	blue
marrón	chestnut, brown
moreno	brown
rosa	pink
violeta	violet
purpúreo	purple
naranja	orange
crema	cream
oscuro	dark
claro	light

◆ Days

lunes	Monday
martes	Tuesday
miércoles	Wednesday
jueves	Thursday
viernes	Friday
sábado	Saturday
domingo	Sunday

◆ Months

enero	January
febrero	February
marzo	March
abril	April
mayo	May
junio	June
julio	July
agosto	August
setiembre	September
octubre	October
noviembre	November
diciembre	December

◆ Seasons

la primavera	spring
el verano	summer
el otoño	autumn
el invierno	winter

◆ Dates

la fecha	date
¿a cuántos estamos?	what's the date?
¿qué fecha es?	what's the date?
estamos a seis de mayo	it's May 6
es el seis de mayo	it's May 6
desde	from
hasta	till
a partir de	from

◆ Time

el segundo	second
el minuto	minute
la hora	hour
el día	day
la semana	week
ocho días	week
dos semanas	fortnight
quince días	fortnight
el mes	month
el año	year
el siglo	century
la mañana	morning
la tarde	afternoon
la noche	night
por la mañana	in the morning
por la tarde	in the afternoon
por la noche	at night
hoy	today
esta noche	tonight
ayer	yesterday
anoche	last night
mañana	tomorrow
mañana por la mañana	tomorrow morning

pasado mañana	the day after tomorrow
el lunes	on Monday
los sábados	on Saturdays
el lunes próximo	next Monday
el lunes pasado	last Monday
esta semana	this week
el fin de semana	(at the) weekend
ahora	now
inmediatamente	immediately
en seguida	straight away
ahora mismo	right now
entonces	then
luego	next
antes (de)	before
después (de)	after
durante	during
temprano	early
tarde	late
pronto	soon
hace dos días	two days ago

◆ Clock

¿qué hora es?	what time is it?
es la una	it's one o'clock
son las dos	it's two o'clock
a las dos	at two o'clock
y cuarto	quarter past
y media	half past
menos cuarto	quarter to
mediodía	noon
medianoche	midnight
de la mañana	a.m.
de la tarde/noche	p.m.
a eso de	about
en punto	exactly, on the dot

◆ Frequency

generalmente	generally
normalmente	normally, usually
a veces	sometimes
muchas veces	often
siempre	always

pocas veces	seldom
rara vez	rarely
nunca	never
todos los días	every day
todos los sábados	every Saturday
una vez	once
dos veces	twice
por día	a day
dos veces por semana	twice a week
otra vez	again
de nuevo	again

◆ Adjectives

muy	very
bastante	quite
fenomenal	great
estupendo	great
fantástico	fantastic
maravilloso	marvellous
agradable	pleasant
bonito	nice
perfecto	perfect
ideal	ideal
excelente	excellent
especial	special
bueno	good
interesante	interesting
horrible	horrible
terrible	terrible
feo	ugly, nasty
fatal	awful
desagradable	unpleasant
malo	bad
aburrido	boring
mejor	better
peor	worse
igual, mismo	same
parecido	similar
limpio	clean
sucio	dirty
barato	cheap

7

caro	expensive
fácil	easy
difícil	difficult
duro	hard
sencillo	simple
práctico	practical
útil	useful
importante	important
justo	fair, just
injusto	unfair, unjust
divertido	enjoyable, funny
emocionante	exciting
tranquilo	peaceful, quiet
ruidoso	noisy
típico	typical
rápido	quick, fast
despacio	slow, slowly

◆ Linking words

y	and
o	or
con	with
sin	without
pero	but
si	if
entonces	then
luego	next
cuando	when
donde	where
por eso	so
porque	because
afortunadamente	fortunately
desafortunadamente	unfortunately
sin embargo	however
rápidamente	quickly
de repente	suddenly

◆ Opinions

sí	yes
no	no
en mi opinión	in my opinion
creo que	I think that
¿qué te parece?	what do you think?

estoy a favor (de)	I'm in favour (of)
es verdad	it's true
es falso	that's not right
tener razón	to be right
no tener razón	to be wrong
estar en contra (de)	to be against
estar equivocado	to be mistaken
gustar	to like
me gusta	I like
no me gusta	I don't like
encantar	to love
me encanta	I love
detestar, odiar	to hate
preferir	to prefer
estar de acuerdo	to agree
¿estás de acuerdo?	do you agree?
sí, estoy de acuerdo	yes, I agree
de acuerdo	agreed
vale	OK

◆ Position words

cerca de	near to
lejos de	far from
al lado de	next to
delante de	in front of
detrás de	behind
enfrente de	opposite
debajo de	under
encima de	above, on top of
en	in, at, on
sobre	on
en el centro de	in the middle of
al fondo de	at the back of
entre	between
hasta	as far as, until
a la izquierda	on the left
a la derecha	on the right
dentro de	inside, within
fuera de	outside
arriba	up, upstairs
abajo	down, downstairs
aquí	here
allí	there
por todas partes	everywhere

◆ Greetings

hola	hello
buenos días	good morning
buenas tardes	good afternoon/ evening
buenas noches	good night
señor	Sir, Mr
señora	Madam, Mrs
señorita	Miss
¿cómo estás?	how are you?
¿qué tal?	how are things?
¿qué hay?	what's up?
¿qué pasa?	what's the matter?
mucho gusto	pleased to meet you
encantado	how do you do?
el gusto es mío	the pleasure is mine
muy bien	very well
por favor	please
gracias	thank you
muchas gracias	thanks a lot
adiós	goodbye
hasta luego	see you soon
pase usted	come in (polite)
pasa	come in (friendly)
siéntese	sit down (polite)
siéntate	sit down (friendly)
bienvenido	welcome
¡estás en tu casa!	feel at home!
tutearse	to address each other as "tú"

◆ Exclamations

salud	cheers
feliz cumpleaños	happy birthday
feliz santo	happy Saint's day
feliz Navidad	happy Christmas
¡felicidades!	best wishes!
¡enhorabuena!	congratulations!
mucha suerte	good luck
igualmente	the same to you
de nada	you're welcome

me da igual	I don't mind
me es igual	it's all the same to me
¡Dios mío!	good heavens!
¡caramba!	gosh!
¡madre mía!	oh dear!
¡ni hablar!	no way! not likely!
¡qué bien!	how good!
¡qué horror!	how awful!
¡qué asco!	how revolting!
¡qué pena!	what a shame!
¡qué lástima!	what a pity!
querido	dear (in a letter)
agradecer	to thank
dar las gracias	to thank
gracias por	thank you for
todo	everything
el abrazo	love from
saludos	best wishes
recuerdos	regards
atentamente	yours faithfully

◆ Asking permission

poder	to be able
molestar	to bother
¿te molesta que...?	do you mind if...?
no quiero molestar	I don't want to be a nuisance
permitir	to allow
¿me permite...?	may I...?
con permiso	if I may
¿es posible...?	is it possible...?
¿sería posible...?	would it be possible...?

◆ Apologising

lo siento mucho	I'm very sorry
lo siento, pero...	I'm sorry but...
¡cuánto lo siento!	I'm so sorry
perdón	sorry
¡te pido perdón!	do forgive me!
fue sin querer	it wasn't meant

School

IN THE CLASSROOM

◆ Foundation words

pasar lista	to call the register	repasar los apuntes	to revise
yo	I'm here	trabajar	to work
presente	present	en limpio	fair copy (in neat)
ausente	absent	en borrador	in rough
siento llegar tarde	sorry I'm late	por ejemplo	for example
levantaos	stand up (to class)	las correcciones	corrections
sentaos	sit down (to class)	el error	mistake
levantar la mano	to put up your hand	la descripción	description
		la frase	sentence
callarse	to keep quiet	la palabra	word
venir	to come	la letra	letter
escuchar	to listen	el acento	accent
mirar	to look	la gramática	grammar
leer	to read	masculino	masculine
escribir	to write	femenino	feminine
buscar	to look for		
sacar	to take out	te toca a ti	it's your turn
abrir	to open	túrnate con tu pareja	take it in turns
cerrar	to close	hacer la entrevista	to do an interview
poner	to put	hacer la encuesta	to do a survey
dejar	to leave	hacer el papel de	to play the part of
decir	to say		
preguntar	to ask	no (lo) sé	I don't know
hacer preguntas	to ask questions	es verdad	it's true
contestar	to answer	es mentira	it's wrong
dibujar	to draw	correcto	correct
diseñar	to sketch	falso	false
copiar	to copy	tener razón	to be right
describir	to describe	no tener razón	to be wrong
corregir	to correct	tengo razón	I'm right
subrayar	to underline	tienes razón	you are right
preparar	to prepare	no tienes razón	you are wrong

◆ Foundation phrases

¡Sacad los cuadernos!	Take out your exercise books!
¡Levantad la mano y contestad!	Put up your hands and answer!
¡Silencio por favor!	Quiet please!
¿Me dejas?	Can you let me have it?
¡Cierra la puerta!	Shut the door!

No entiendo.	I don't understand.
¡Repite por favor!	Repeat please!
¿Cómo se escribe?	How is it spelled?
¿Puedes deletrearlo?	Can you spell it out?
¿Hablas inglés?	Do you speak English?
¿Cómo se dice... en español?	How do you say... in Spanish?
¿Qué es... en inglés?	What is... in English?
¿Qué significa?	What does it mean?
¿Qué quiere decir?	What does it mean?
¿Cómo se pronuncia?	How is it pronounced?

◆ **Higher words**

You might also need these words:

		Add any other useful words here:
explicar	to explain	
pronunciar	to pronounce	....
pedir prestado	to borrow	
esforzarse	to make an effort	....
comportarse	to behave	
desobedecer	to disobey	....
la regla	rule	
regañar	to tell off	....

CLASSROOM OBJECTS

◆ **Foundation words**

la cartera	school bag	el ordenador	computer
el estuche	pencil case	el computador	computer
el bolígrafo (boli)	biro	la televisión	television
el lápiz	pencil	el televisor	television set
el rotulador	felt-tipped pen	el retroprojector	OHP
la regla	ruler	la mesa	table
el sacapuntas	pencil sharpener	la silla	chair
la goma (de borrar)	rubber	la puerta	door
las tijeras	scissors	la ventana	window
el disquete	disc		
la calculadora	calculator	el diccionario	dictionary
		la página	page
la pizarra	board	la cinta	tape
la tiza	chalk	la cassette	cassette
el papel	paper	la casete	cassette
el cuaderno	exercise book	el compás	compass
el libro (de texto)	text book	el mapa	map

11

THE TIMETABLE

◆ Foundation words

ir al colegio	to go to school	útil	useful
estudiar	to study	obligatorio	compulsory
aprender	to learn	práctico	practical
enseñar	to teach		
		inteligente	intelligent
la asignatura	subject	torpe	not very bright
el idioma	language	severo	strict
el español	Spanish		
el francés	French	empezar	to start
el alemán	German	terminar	to finish
el inglés	English	durar	to last
las ciencias	science		
la biología	biology	la clase	class
la física	physics	la lección	lesson
la química	chemistry	los estudios	studies
las matemáticas	maths	el curso	course
la informática	computer studies	el horario	timetable
la geografía	geography		
la historia	history	llevar	to wear
la religión	religious studies	el uniforme	uniform
el dibujo	art	el recreo	break
el drama	drama	la hora de comer	dinner time
la música	music	después de las clases	after school
la cocina	food studies		
la corte y confección	textiles	los deberes	homework
la tecnología	technology	la nota	mark
los trabajos manuales	CDT	sacar buenas notas	to get good marks
la educación física	PE	sacar malas notas	to get bad marks
los deportes	sport	aprobar	to pass
la gimnasia	gymnastics	suspender	to fail
la ética	ethics	la prueba	test
la lengua	Spanish language	el examen	exam
		el proyecto	project
fácil	easy	el esfuerzo	effort
difícil	difficult	examinarse de	to take an exam
duro	hard	el resultado	result
estupendo	great		
interesante	interesting		
aburrido	boring		
aburrirse	to be (get) bored		

◆ Foundation phrases

¿Cúantas asignaturas estudias?	How many subjects do you study?
Estudio siete: matemáticas, inglés...	I study seven: maths, English...
Me gusta el español.	I like Spanish.
No me gusta nada la geografía.	I don't like geography at all.
Me gustan las ciencias.	I like science.
No me gustan las matemáticas.	I don't like maths.
Me encantan los idiomas.	I love languages.
Creo que las ciencias son muy útiles.	I think that science is very useful.
Estoy fuerte/flojo en...	I'm good/weak at...
Las clases empiezan a las nueve y diez y terminan a las tres y veinticinco.	Classes start at 9.10 a.m. and finish at 3.25 p.m.
Hay cinco clases por día.	There are five lessons a day.
Las lecciones duran una hora.	Lessons last one hour.
Durante el recreo juego al fútbol o charlo con mis amigos.	During break I play football or chat to my friends.
Tengo que llevar uniforme.	I have to wear a uniform.
Hago mis deberes a las siete.	I do my homework at seven o'clock.

◆ Higher words

You might also need these words.

explicar	to explain
pedir prestado	to borrow
confiscar	to confiscate
opinar	to think of
clasificar	to classify
los clases de repaso	revision classes
repetir curso	to repeat a year
el año académico	academic year
la aptitud	ability

Add any other useful words here:

....

....

....

....

....

◆ Higher phrases

¿Cuánto tiempo hace que aprendes el español?	How long have you been learning Spanish?
Hace tres años que lo aprendo.	I've been learning it for three years.
En mi opinión las clases son demasiado largas.	In my opinion lessons are too long.
¿Qué opinas del uniforme?	What do you think of the uniform?
Se me da muy bien la historia.	I'm very good at history.
Se me da mal la física.	I'm weak in physics.
La encuentro difícil y pesado.	I find it hard and boring.
Las matemáticas me traen frito.	Maths just defeats me.

13

AT SCHOOL

◆ Foundation words

la escuela	primary school
el colegio	secondary school
el cole	(up to 14)
el instituto	secondary school (14–18)
el alumno	pupil (m)
la alumna	pupil (f)
el/la estudiante	student
el profesor	teacher (m)
la profesora	teacher (f)
el director	headteacher (m)
la directora	headteacher (f)
el aula (f)	classroom

la biblioteca	library
la cantina	canteen
el gimnasio	gym
el laboratorio	laboratory
la sala de actos	hall
el salón de actos	assembly room
el patio	yard, playground
el pasillo	corridor
portarse bien	to behave well
portarse mal	to behave badly
charlar	to chat
castigar	to punish
el castigo	punishment
el club	club

◆ Higher words

You might also need these words:

el taller	workshop
la sala de profesores	staffroom
el vestuario	changing room
privado	private
mixto	mixed
del estado	state
el trimestre	term
el simestre	6-month term
comprensivo	understanding
exigente	demanding
educar	to educate
los exámenes parciales	modular exams
la educación preescolar	nursery education
la EGB	(age 6–14)
(Educación General Básica)	
la FP	(age 14+)
(Formación Profesional)	
el BUP	(age 14–17)
(Bachillerato Unificado y Polivalente)	
el COU	(age 17+)
(Curso de Orientación Universitaria	

Add any other useful words here:

....

....

....

....

....

....

....

....

....

....

EXAM LANGUAGE

Pon una equis en la casilla correcta.	Put a cross in the correct box.
Pon una señal al lado de sólo 5 letras	Tick only 5 letters.
Pon un número en la casilla.	Put a number in the box.
Pon en orden.	Put in order.
Marca con una x.	Mark with a x.
Indica si la frase es verdadero [✓], falso [✗] o no sabes [?].	Indicate if the sentence is true [✓], false [✗] or you don't know [?].
Indica los errores.	Point out the mistakes.
Indica con los números de 1 a 5 el orden correcto.	Indicate the correct order using the numbers 1–5.
Contesta a las preguntas.	Answer the questions.
Contesta "sí" o "no" a las preguntas siguientes.	Answer the following questions with "yes" or "no".
Contesta todas las preguntas.	Answer all the questions.
Rellena las casillas.	Fill in the boxes.
Rellena los detalles siguientes.	Fill in the following details.
Rellena los detalles en español.	Fill in the details in Spanish.
Rellena los huecos con...	Fill in the gaps with...
Rellena los espacios con una palabra de la lista.	Fill in the spaces with a word from the list
Rellena la tabla con la información correcta.	Fill in the table with the correct information.
Rellena el formulario.	Fill in the form.
Da la información necesaria.	Give the necessary information.
Da razones.	Give reasons.
Da tu opinión sobre...	Give your opinion on...
Da la vuelta.	Turn over.
Escoge la frase correcta para cada dibujo.	Choose the right phrase for each drawing.
Empareja los símbolos con las personas.	Match the symbols to the people.
Escribe la letra/el número	Write the letter/number.
Escribe los nombres.	Write the names.
Escribe un artículo/una carta/una postal.	Write an article/a letter/a postcard.
Incluye la siguiente información.	Include the following information.
Incluye tantos detalles y opiniones como puedas.	Include as many details and opinions as you can.
Lee este folleto.	Read this brochure.
Escucha este cassette.	Listen to this cassette.
Escucha esta conversación.	Listen to this conversation.
Escucha esta entrevista.	Listen to this interview.
Escucha este mensaje.	Listen to this message.
No se necesitan todas las letras/palabras.	You don't need all the letters/words.

SCHOOL

abre	open	encuentra	find
añade	add	estudia	study
busca	look for	explica	explain
cambia	change	haz un resumen	make a summary
cierra	close	haz una comparación	make a comparison
compara	compare		
completa	complete	haz una lista	make a list
convence	convince	imagina	imagine
copia	copy	justifica tu opinión	justify your opinion
decide	decide		
describe	describe	menciona	mention
dibuja	draw	subraya	underline
diseña	sketch	sugiere	suggest

◆ **Ejercicio**

Unjumble the letters to make eight school subjects.
Try to do this exercise without looking back.

1. SENIACIC ....

2. JOBUDI ....

3. GILENS ....

4. ICCANO ....

5. THARIOSI ....

6. MANLEA ....

7. SAMICU ....

8. GORENILI ....

(Answer on page 96)

Home Life

HOUSEWORK

◆ Foundation words

ayudar	to help	fregar los platos	to do the washing up
las faenas de casa	housework, chores	poner la mesa	to set the table
los quehaceres	household jobs	preparar la comida	to prepare the food (meal)
hacer los quehaceres	to do household jobs	cocinar	to cook
pasar la aspiradora	to vacuum	hacer las camas	to make the beds
quitar el polvo	to dust	hacer la compra	to do the shopping
limpiar	to clean	lavar el coche	to wash the car
arreglar	to tidy	cuidar el jardín	to do the gardening
barrer	to sweep		
planchar	to iron		

◆ Foundation phrases

¿Ayudas a tus padres en casa?	Do you help your parents in the house?
Generalmente lavo los platos y hago mi cama.	I usually do the washing up and make my bed.
Los fines de semana hago la compra con mi padre.	At weekends I do the shopping with my dad.
A veces paso la aspiradora.	I sometimes do the vacuuming.

◆ Higher words

You might also need these words:

regar las plantas	to water the plants
cortar la hierba	to cut the grass
dar de comer al perro	to feed the dog
ordenar	to tidy up
hacer la colada	to do the washing

Add any other useful words here:

....

....

◆ Higher phrases

¿Quieres que te eche una mano?	Do you want me to give you a hand?
¿Puedo ayudarte a fregar los platos?	Can I help you to wash the dishes?
Mi padre no hace nada para ayudar en casa.	My dad does nothing to help in the house.
No saldrás a jugar hasta que ordenes tu habitación.	You can't go out till you've tidied up your room.
Pon la mesa y siéntate a comer.	Set the table and sit down to eat.
Cuido a los niños cuando mis padres salen.	I look after the children when my parents go out.
En el verano corto la hierba.	I cut the grass in summer.

DAILY ROUTINE

◆ Foundation words

levantarse	to get up	estar en casa	to be in the house
acostarse	to go to bed	soler	to be in the habit of
dormirse	to go to sleep		
lavarse	to get washed	la secadora	hair dryer
lavarse la cabeza	to wash your hair	el champú	shampoo
lavarse los dientes	to clean your teeth	el papel higiénico	toilet paper
ducharse	to have a shower	el cepillo	brush
afeitarse	to shave	el cepillo de dientes	tooth brush
peinarse	to comb your hair	la pasta de dientes	tooth paste
arreglarse	to get ready	el espejo	mirror
vestirse	to get dressed	el jabón	soap
quitarse la ropa	to get undressed	la toalla	towel

◆ Foundation phrases

¿A qué hora te levantas normalmente?	What time do you normally get up?
Me levanto a las ocho menos cuarto.	I get up at quarter to eight.
¿Qué haces después?	What do you do next?
Me lavo y me peino.	I get washed and comb my hair.
Me ducho antes de vestirme.	I have a shower before getting dressed.
¿A qué hora te acuestas?	What time do you go to bed?
Suelo acostarme a las diez y media.	I usually go to bed at half past ten.
¿Puedo ducharme?	Can I have a shower?
¿Puedo tomar un baño?	Can I have a bath?
Normalmente desayuno a las ocho.	I usually have breakfast at eight o'clock.
¿A qué hora cenas?	What time do you have supper?

◆ Higher words

You might also need these words:

secarse	to dry yourself
la esponja	sponge
el paño	flannel
compartir	to share

Add any other useful words here:

....

....

◆ Higher phrases

No me gusta cenar tarde.	I don't like to eat late at night.
Me cuesta mucho digerir la comida.	It's difficult to digest food.
Preferimos ir de tapeo que ir a comer a los restaurantes.	We prefer to eat snack food rather than go to eat at a restaurant.
Solemos comer pollo los domingos.	We usually eat chicken on Sundays.
Tengo que compartir mi dormitorio.	I have to share my bedroom.

THE HOUSE

◆ Foundation words

vivir	to live	la cocina	kitchen
el piso	flat	el comedor	dining room
la casa	house	el salón	living room
la casa adosada	semi-detached	el dormitorio	bedroom
el chalet	detached, cottage	el cuarto de baño	bathroom
la granja	farm	el wáter, el lavabo	toilet
		el balcón	balcony
cómodo	comfortable	el patio	patio
incómodo	uncomfortable	la terraza	terrace
moderno	modern	el desván	loft, attic
antiguo	old	el tejado	roof
grande	big	el pasillo	corridor
pequeño	small	la escalera	stairs
		el garaje	garage
la habitación	room	el jardín	garden
la planta baja	ground floor	la ventana	window
el primer piso	first floor	la puerta	door
arriba	upstairs	la calefacción central	central heating
abajo	downstairs	el radiador	radiator

◆ Foundation phrases

¿Puedes describir tu casa?	Can you describe your house?
Mi casa es bastante grande y cómoda.	My house is quite big and comfortable.
Está pintado de blanco.	It's painted white.
¿Cuántos cuartos hay?	How many rooms are there?
¿Cómo es tu dormitorio?	What's your bedroom like?
Es pequeño pero es cómodo.	It's small but comfortable.
Comparto mi dormitorio con mi hermano menor.	I share my bedroom with my younger brother.
Mi dormitorio da al jardín.	My bedroom looks out on to the garden.

◆ Higher words

You might also need these words:

el bloque de viviendas	block of flats
instalarse	to settle (in)
mudarse	to move house
el sótano	basement
el azulejo	glazed tile
la teja	roof tile
de ladrillo	made of brick

Add any other useful words here:

....

....

....

HOUSE CONTENTS

◆ Foundation words

la cocina de gas	gas cooker	la chimenea	fireplace
la cocina eléctrica	electric cooker	las cortinas	curtains
el horno	oven	el cuadro	picture
el fregadero	sink	la librería	bookcase
el frigorífico	fridge	el reloj	clock
la nevera	fridge		
el congelador	freezer	la cama	bed
la lavadora	washing machine	el armario	cupboard
el lavaplatos	dishwasher	el guardarropa	wardrobe
el taburete	stool	el tocador	dressing table
el estante	shelf	la mesilla de noche	bedside table
la estantería	shelf	la cómoda	chest of drawers
		el pupitre	desk
la mesa	table	la lámpara	lamp
la silla	chair	el despertador	alarm clock
los muebles	furniture	la almohada	pillow
la alfombra	rug, carpet	la manta	blanket
la moqueta	fitted carpet	la sábana	sheet
el sofá, el canapé	sofa	el colchón	mattress
la butaca, el sillón	armchair	la pared	wall
		el póster	poster
el televisor	television set		
el vídeo	video	el baño	bath
el tocadiscos	record player	el lavabo	wash basin
la radio	radio	el grifo	tap
el equipo de música	hi-fi system	la ducha	shower

◆ Higher words

You might also need these words:

amueblado	furnished
la contraventana	shutter
las persianas	blinds
la valla	fence
la tapia	garden wall
el estanque	pond
el lavavajillas	dishwasher
el microondas	microwave oven
el cuarto de estar	living room
el cojín	cushion
el papel pintado	wallpaper

Add any other useful words here:

....

....

....

....

....

Health

WELL-BEING

◆ Foundation words

la salud	health	tener miedo	to be frightened
estar...	to be...	tener sueño	to be sleepy
bien	well	encontrarse bien	to feel well
regular	OK	encontrarse mal	to feel bad
mal	bad		
enfermo	ill	la enfermedad	illness
mareado	sick	la tos	cough
fatal	awful	ronco	hoarse
herido	injured, hurt	el mareo	sea/travel sickness
muerto	dead	el catarro	cold
mejor	better	la gripe	flu
peor	worse	SIDA	AIDS
cansado	tired	el dolor de cabeza	headache
sentirse mal	to feel ill	toser	to cough
estar resfriado	to have a cold	fumar	to smoke
estar constipado	to have a cold	vomitar	to vomit, be sick
tener fiebre	to have a temperature	desmayarse	to faint, swoon
		marearse	to feel sick, dizzy
tener calor	to be hot	sudar	to sweat
tener frío	to be cold	temblar	to tremble
tener hambre	to be hungry	doler	to hurt
tener sed	to be thirsty		

◆ Foundation phrases

Me duele la cabeza.	I've got a headache.
Tengo dolor de muelas.	I've got toothache.
¿Cómo estás?	How are you?
¿Qué te pasa?	What's the matter with you?
¿Estás enfermo?	Are you ill?
Estoy resfriado y tengo la tos.	I've got a cold and a cough.
No fumo. Es malo para la salud.	I don't smoke. It's bad for your health.

PARTS OF THE BODY

◆ Foundation words

la cara	face	el pecho	chest
la frente	forehead	el corazón	heart
el ojo	eye	el estómago, el vientre	stomach
la boca	mouth	el brazo	arm
los labios	lips	la mano	hand
el diente	tooth	la muñeca	wrist
la nariz	nose	el dedo	finger
la oreja	ear	la pierna	leg
la garganta	throat	el muslo	thigh
la mejilla	cheek	la rodilla	knee
el cuerpo	body	el tobillo	ankle
el cuello	neck	el pie	foot
la espalda	back	el dedo del pie	toe

ILLNESS AND TREATMENT

◆ Foundation words

la farmacia	chemist's	la aspirina	aspirin
la Cruz Roja	Red Cross	la crema	cream
la clínica	clinic	la medicina	medicine
la consulta	(doctor's) surgery, examination	el jarabe para la tos	cough medicine
el consultorio	consulting room	la pastilla	tablet
el tratamiento	treatment	el comprimido	pill, tablet
el remedio	remedy	la tirita	sticky plaster
la receta	prescription	la venda	bandage
la inyección	injection	el tampón	tampon
embarazada	pregnant	el paño higiénico	sanitary towel
		la cucharada	spoonful
necesitar	to need	el accidente	accident
tomar	to take	la herida	wound, injury
vendar	to bandage	sufrir	to suffer
examinar	to examine	caerse	to fall
tomar la temperatura	to take the temperature	ahogarse	to drown
		quemarse	to burn yourself
aconsejar	to advise	la quemadura	burn
mejorarse	to get better	romperse	to break
guardar cama	to stay in bed	el hueso	bone
proteger	to protect	la sangre	blood
evitar	to avoid	la piel	skin

llamar a la ambulancia	to call an ambulance	la quemadura del sol	sunburn
llamar al médico	to call the doctor	picar	to sting, bite
grave	serious	la picadura	sting, bite
urgente	urgent	la abeja	bee
urgencias	casualty dept	la avispa	wasp
el hospital	hospital	morder	to bite

◆ Foundation phrases

¡Ay!	Ouch!
¡Cuidado!	Be careful!
¡Ojo!	Watch out!
¡Socorro!	Help!
Quiero unas aspirinas por favor.	I'd like some aspirins please.
Creo que me he roto la pierna.	I think that I've broken my leg.

◆ Higher words

You might also need these words:

hacer ejercicio físico	to exercise	la fibra (diatética)	(dietary) fibre
el físico	physique	la proteína	protein
fisicamente	physically	estar bien de salud	to be in good health
el régimen	diet		
estar a régimen	to be on a diet	esforzarse	to exert yourself
adelgazar	to lose weight	dejar de fumar	to stop smoking
engordar	to put on weight	el humo	smoke
comer grasas	to eat fatty foods	el cáncer de pulmón	lung cancer
los alimentos bajos en calorías	low-fat foods	el fumar pasivo	passive-smoking
		el gran fumador	heavy smoker
los alimentos naturales	health foods	la droga	drug
la comida sana	wholesome food	peligroso	dangerous
la comida basura	junk food	dañoso	harmful
la vitamina	vitamin	la bebida alcohólica	alcoholic drink

emborracharse	to get drunk	*Add any other useful words here:*
alcohólico	alcoholic	
pedir hora	to make an appointment	....
la diarrea	diarrhoea	....
estreñido	constipated	
hinchado	swollen	....
torcerse	to twist, sprain	
estar torcido	to be twisted	....
tener alergía a	to be allergic to	
el antibiótico	antibiotic	....
la pomada	ointment	
padecer de	to suffer from	....
el estrés	stress	
trasplantar	to transplant	....
el trasplante de corazón	heart transplant	
el trasplante hepático	liver transplant	....
sacar	to take out	
empastar	to fill	....
el empaste	filling	

◆ Higher phrases

Hago mucho ejercicio físico.	I do a lot of physical exercise.
No me repugna tomar algo de vez en cuando.	I'm not averse to an occasional drink.
En mi opinión el fumar pasivo es malísimo.	In my opinion passive smoking is appalling.
Quisiera pedir hora cuanto antes.	I'd like to make an appointment as soon as possible.
¿Puede darme hora con...?	Can you give me an appointment with...?
Me he torcido el tobillo.	I've sprained my ankle.
Padece del corazón.	He has heart trouble.

Food

MEALS

◆ Foundation words

la comida	food, meal	picante	spicy
el desayuno	breakfast	el sabor	taste, flavour
la comida	lunch	el olor	smell
el almuerzo	lunch	oler a	to smell of
la merienda	snack, tea		
la cena	supper	probar	to try
merendar	to have a snack	un poco	a bit
		mucho	a lot
delicioso	delicious	más	more
rico	tasty	nada más	no more
dulce	sweet	bastante	sufficient, enough
salado	salty	¡basta!	that's enough!

FRUIT AND VEGETABLES

◆ Foundation words

las frutas	fruit	las verduras	vegetables
la manzana	apple	la lechuga	lettuce
la pera	pear	el pepino	cucumber
la cereza	cherry	el pimiento rojo	red pepper
la ciruela	plum	el pimiento verde	green pepper
el melocotón	peach	el ajo	garlic
el albaricoque	apricot	la cebolla	onion
la naranja	orange	los guisantes	peas
el limón	lemon	las habas	broad beans
el higo	fig	las judías verdes	green beans
la fresa	strawberry	la col	cabbage
la frambuesa	raspberry	las coles de Bruselas	Brussels sprouts
el plátano	banana	la coliflor	cauliflower
la piña	pineapple	las patatas	potatoes
el pomelo	grapefruit	la zanahoria	carrot
las uvas	grapes	los champiñones	mushrooms
la sandía	water melon	el espárrago	asparagus
el tomate	tomato	las aceitunas	olives

◆ Higher words

You might also need these words:

el aguacate	avocado	la alcachofa	artichoke
la granada	pomegranate	los garbanzos	chick-peas
		la berenjena	aubergine

FOOD STUFFS

◆ Foundation words

el pan	bread	el café	café, coffee
el pan de molde	loaf	la cafetería	café
la barra de pan	French stick	el bar	bar
el panecillo	roll	la hamburguesería	hamburger restaurant
el bollo	roll, bun		
la tostada	piece of toast		
la mantequilla	butter	la tapa	bar snack
la mermelada	jam	la porción	very small portion
el bocadillo	sandwich	la ración (de)	large portion (of)
los churros	Spanish doughnuts	dos raciones (de)	two portions (of)
las patatas fritas	crisps, chips	la hamburguesa	hamburger
el pastel	cake	la hamburguesa de queso	cheeseburger
la galleta	biscuit		
el bizcocho	sponge cake	el perrito caliente	hot dog
el chocolate	chocolate	la pizza	pizza
el turrón	nougat	los caramelos	sweets

¡BUEN PROVECHO!

PIZZA-PIZZA

servicio gratuito a domicilio.
Pizzas recién hechas.
En tu casa, en menos de 30 minutos

— M E N U —

MARGARITA	Queso y tomate.
VEGETAL	Queso, tomate, champiñones, pimiento verde, aceitunas y cebolla.
HAWAIANA	Piña y jámon.
PIAMONTESA	Salami, bacon, champiñones.
PICANTE	Carne, guindilla y salsa picante.
RODEO	Carne, bacon y salsa barbacoa.
BOLOGNESA	Queso, tomate, carne y cebolla.
ATLANTICA	Atún, cebolla, aceitunas verdes, queso y tomate.

◆ Foundation words

la sopa	soup	los mejillones	mussels
la ensalada	salad	las gambas	prawns
la ensalada mixta	mixed salad	la langosta	lobster
el gazpacho	gazpacho	el cangrejo	crab
el salchichón	salami		
		el postre	dessert, sweet
el plato combinado	combined dish	el helado	ice-cream
las carnes	meats	la tarta	cake, tart
la carne de cerdo	pork	el flan	caramel cream
la carne de cordero	lamb	el queso	cheese
la carne de ternera	veal	el yogur	yogurt
la carne de vaca	beef	la nata	cream
el pollo	chicken	la fruta fresca	fresh fruit
el pavo	turkey		
el pato	duck	las bebidas	drinks
el jamón de york	boiled ham	el té	tea
el jamón serrano	cured ham	el café	coffee
la salchicha	sausage	la taza de café	cup of coffee
el bistec	steak	el café solo	black coffee
el filete	fillet steak	el café con leche	white coffee
la chuleta	chop	el chocolate (caliente)	(hot) chocolate
la chuleta de cerdo	pork chop	el refresco	cold (iced) drink
el solomillo	sirloin	el agua (f)	water
el cocido	stew	el agua mineral	mineral water
		con gas/sin gas	carbonated/still
asado	roast	la cola	cola
a la plancha	grilled	la limonada	lemonade
frito	fried	la gaseosa	lemonade
		la naranjada	orangeade
el arroz	rice	la leche	milk
los huevos	eggs	el zumo de fruta	fruit juice
la tortilla	omelette	el zumo de naranja	fresh orange juice
		el coñac	brandy
el pescado	fish	la ginebra	gin
el bacalao	cod	el jerez	sherry
la merluza	hake	la manzanilla	dry pale sherry
el lenguado	sole	el champán	champagne
el rape	angler fish	la cerveza	beer
las sardinas	sardines	la sidra	cider
el atún	tuna	el vino blanco	white wine
la trucha	trout	el vino tinto	red wine
los calamares	squid	el vino rosado	rosé wine
los mariscos	shellfish	la sangría	sangría

el azúcar	sugar	la mayonesa	mayonnaise
la sal	salt	el aceite (de oliva)	(olive) oil
la pimienta	pepper	la mostaza	mustard
el vinagre	vinegar	la salsa	sauce

◆ Foundation phrases

Mi comida favorita es el pollo.	My favourite food is chicken.
Me gustan mucho las hamburguesas.	I like hamburgers a lot.
Me encanta el arroz.	I love rice.
Detesto las aceitunas.	I hate olives.
Lo siento pero no me gusta.	I'm sorry but I don't like it.
Para el desayuno tomo el café con leche y pan tostado.	At breakfast I have white coffee and toast.
Tengo preferencia por...	I prefer...
No me apetece...	I don't fancy...
Soy vegeteriano/vegeteriana.	I'm a vegetarian.
Me hace falta...	I need...

◆ Higher words

You might also need these words:

los espaguetis	spaghetti	insalubre	unhealthy
las albóndigas	meat balls	apetitoso	appetising, tasty
el lomo	loin	riquísimo	exceptionally tasty
la almeja	clam	soso	tasteless, unsalted
el boquerón	anchovy	repugnar	to disgust, revolt
la caña	glass of beer		
el pan integral	wholemeal bread		
el café descafeinado	decaffeinated coffee	*Add any other useful words here:*	
la leche entera	full fat milk		
la leche desnatada	skimmed milk		
la sal marina	sea salt		
la miel	honey		
las nueces	nuts		
crudo	raw		
cocido	cooked		
poco hecho	rare		
muy hecho	well-done		
amargo	bitter		
sano	wholesome, good		
saludable	healthy		

....

....

....

....

....

....

....

....

AT A RESTAURANT

◆ Foundation words

Spanish	English	Spanish	English
déme... por favor	give me... please	el aperitivo	aperitif
traígame... por favor	bring me... please	los entremeses	starters
tráiganos... por favor	bring us... please	el plato principal	main course
¿qué es...?	what is...?		
¡oíga!	hey! (to waiter)	el mantel	tablecloth
¡salud!	cheers!	la servilleta	serviette
recomendar	to recommend	el cuchillo	knife
sugerir	to suggest	el tenedor	fork
		la cuchara	spoon
el restaurante	restaurant	el vaso	glass
el restaurante autoservicio	self-service restaurant	la jarra	mug, jug
		la taza	cup
reservar	to reserve	el plato	plate
la reserva	reservation	el platillo	saucer
la mesa	table	faltar	to be missing
libre	free		
para 3 personas	for 3 people	la cuenta	bill
servir	to serve, wait on	el servicio	service charge
el camarero	waiter	incluido	included
la camarera	waitress	IVA	VAT
el menú	menu	la propina	tip
el menú del día	fixed price meal	aceptar	to accept
la carta	à la carte menu	la tarjeta de crédito	credit card
el plato del día	dish of the day	el error	mistake

◆ Foundation phrases

Somos cinco.	There are five of us.
Quisiera una mesa para dos personas.	I'd like a table for two.
Tengo la mesa reservada en la terraza.	I have a table reserved on the terrace.
¿Qué recomienda?	What do you recommend?
¿Qué desea?	What are you going to have?
¿Y para beber?	And to drink?
¡Qué aproveche!	Enjoy your meal!
Falta un tenedor.	There's a fork missing.
¿Dónde está el teléfono?	Where's the phone?
¿Dónde están los servicios?	Where are the toilets?
Deme una cocacola por favor.	Give me a cola, please.
Quiero el menú de 1400 pesetas.	I'd like the 1400 peseta menu.
¿Me puede decir qué es el cocido?	Can you tell me what "cocido" is?
Para empezar voy a tomar sopa.	I'll have soup to start.
Estaba muy rico/estupendo.	It was delicious/great.

◆ Higher words

You might also need these words:

Add any other useful words here:

quedarse satisfecho	to be full
atestarse	to stuff yourself
la especialidad	speciality
la receta	recipe
cortar	to cut
pelar	to peel
agitar	to stir
batir	to beat
mezclar	to mix
añadir	to add
sazonar	to season
quejarse	to complain

....

....

....

....

....

....

◆ Higher phrases

Está en su punto.	It's done to a turn.
¡Esto no se puede consentir!	It's just not good enough!
Me repugna la idea de comer carne.	The idea of eating meat revolts me.
No puedo más.	I'm full (up).
Quiero quejarme, la sopa está fría.	I wish to complain, the soup is cold.
Voy a formular la queja.	I'm going to make a formal complaint.
La camarera estuvo muy antipática.	The waitress was very rude.
¿El servicio está incluido?	Is the service charge included?
¡Quédese con la vuelta!	Keep the change!

Personal Life

PERSONAL DETAILS

◆ Foundation words

presentar	to introduce	el cumpleaños	birthday
presentarse	to introduce yourself	el santo	Saint's day
la identidad	identity	la fecha de nacimiento	date of birth
el carnet de identidad	identity card	el lugar de nacimiento	place of birth
		nací	I was born
el número	number	la nacionalidad	nationality
la calle	street	soy	I am
el número de teléfono	phone number	inglés/inglesa	English
		escocés/escocesa	Scottish
llamarse	to be called	irlandés/irlandesa	Irish
mi, mis	my	galés/galesa	Welsh
el nombre	first name	británico/británica	British
el apellido	surname	alemán/alemana	German
se escribe	it is spelled	francés/francesa	French
deletrear	to spell out	español/española	Spanish
la edad	age		
cumplir... años	to be ... years old		

For more nationalities and countries, see page 71.

◆ Foundation phrases

Me voy a presentar.	I'm going to introduce myself.
Me llamo Karen y tengo quince años.	My name is Karen and I'm 15 years old.
¿Cómo se escribe?	How do you spell it?
Soy escocesa.	I'm Scottish.
Nací en Edimburgo.	I was born in Edinburgh.
Tengo 14 años.	I'm 14 years old.
¿Cuántos años tienes?	How old are you?
Mi dirección es...	My address is...

Fill in your details:

Nombre _____

Apellido _____

La fecha de nacimiento _____

El lugar de nacimiento _____

Nacionalidad _____

DESCRIPTIONS

◆ **Foundation words**

describir	to describe	cortés (cortesa)	polite
la descripción	description	trabajador	hard-working
		aplicado	studious
alto	tall	ambicioso	ambitious
bajo	small	perezoso	lazy
gordo	fat	formal	well-behaved
delgado	thin	travieso	naughty
flaco	skinny	listo	clever
grueso	stout, thick-set	inteligente	intelligent
guapo	good-looking	capaz	capable
feo	ugly	estúpido, tonto	stupid, silly
moreno	dark-skinned	loco	mad
pálido	pale	alegre	happy
jóven	young	divertido, gracioso	amusing
viejo	old	triste	sad
		cómico	funny
el pelo	hair	animado	lively
largo	long	serio	serious
corto	short	ruidoso	noisy
rizado	curly	hablador	talkative
liso	straight	callado	quiet
castaño	brown	abierto	open
rubio	fair, blond	sensible	sensitive
ser pelirrojo	to be a redhead	tímido	shy
calvo	bald	nervioso	nervous
la barba	beard	inocente	innocent, naive
el bigote	moustache	elegante	smart
llevar	to wear	quieto, tranquilo	calm, placid
las gafas	glasses	agresivo	aggressive
las lentillas	contact lenses	paciente	patient
la cara	face	impaciente	impatient
redondo	round	rico	rich
cuadrado	square	pobre	poor
la calidad	quality	honrado	honest
simpático	nice	responsable	responsible
antipático	nasty, unpleasant	goloso	greedy
amable	kind		
cariñoso	affectionate	conocido	well-known
generoso	generous	famoso	famous

popular	popular	cobarde	coward(ly)
optimista	optimistic	deportista	sporty
pesimista	pessimistic	orgulloso	proud
fuerte	strong	sordo	deaf
débil	weak	ciego	blind
valiente	brave	cojo	crippled
atrevido	daring		

◆ Foundation phrases

Tengo el pelo negro y corto y los ojos verdes.	I've got short, black hair and green eyes.
Soy bastante alta y habladora.	I'm quite tall and chatty.

◆ Higher words

You might also need these words:

pesar	to weigh	enérgico	energetic
medir	to measure	dinámico	dynamic
parecido a	similar to	extrovertido	extrovert(ed)
de estatura regular	of medium height	introvertido	introvert(ed)
pelinegro	black-haired	artístico	artistic
pelirrubio	fair-haired	ordenado	organised
el flequillo	fringe	insoportable	unbearable
la peca	freckle	celoso	jealous
el tatuaje	tattoo	terco	stubborn
ponerse colorado	to blush	egoísta	selfish
bronceado	tanned	pesado	boring
marchoso	trendy		
mono	dishy	*Add any other useful words here:*	
majo	nice, attractive		

el carácter	character
amistoso	friendly
sofisticado	sophisticated
seguro de mí mismo	self-confident
independiente	independent
inseguro	self-conscious

....

....

....

....

◆ Higher phrases

Me parezco a...	I look like...
¿A quién te pareces?	Who do you look like?
Peso cincuenta y siete kilos.	I weigh 57 kilos.
Mido un metro setenta y cinco.	I measure 1 metre 75.
Nací en mil novecientos ochenta.	I was born in 1980.

33

FAMILY

◆ Foundation words

la familia	family	el esposo, el marido	husband
los padres	parents	la esposa, la mujer	wife
el padre	father	la pareja	couple
papá	dad	el amigo/la amiga	friend
la madre	mother	el nieto	grandson
mamá	mum	la nieta	grand-daughter
el hermano	brother	el yerno	son-in-law
la hermana	sister	la yerna	daughter-in-law
el hijo	son	el suegro	father-in-law
la hija	daughter	la suegra	mother-in-law
los hijos	children		
el niño/la niña	child	la boda	wedding
gemelo	twin	el novio	fiancé
los parientes	relatives	la novia	fiancée
los abuelos	grandparents	soltero	single
el abuelo	grandfather	casado	married
la abuela	grandmother	casarse con	to marry
el tío	uncle	divorciado	divorced
la tía	aunt	divorciarse	to get divorced
el primo/la prima	cousin	viudo	widowed
el sobrino	nephew	estar muerto	to be dead
la sobrina	niece	morir	to die

◆ Foundation phrases

¿Cúantas personas hay en tu familia?	How many people are in your family?
Hay cuatro personas.	There are four people.
Soy hijo único.	I'm an only child.
También tengo un perro moreno que se llama Flash.	I've also got a brown dog called Flash.
Mi amigo/amiga se llama...	My friend is called...

◆ Higher words

You might also need these words:

conocerse	to meet	el cuñado	brother-in-law
enamorarse de	to fall in love with	la cuñada	sister-in-law
vivir juntos	to live together	jubilado	retired
la relación	relationship	jubilarse	to retire
el matrimonio	married couple		
amar, querer	to love	*Add any other useful words here:*	
llevarse bien con	to get on well with		
aguantar	to put up with	....	
echar de menos	to miss (someone)		
separarse de	to separate from	....	
el bebé	baby		

PETS AND ANIMALS

◆ Foundation words

el animal doméstico	pet	el periquito	budgie
el perro	dog	la jaula	cage
el gato	cat	el caballo	horse
el hamster	hamster	el burro	donkey
el conejo	rabbit	la vaca	cow
el ratón	mouse	la oveja	sheep
la tortuga	tortoise	la cabra	goat
el pez	fish	el toro	bull
el pájaro	bird	la gallina	hen

◆ Higher words

You might also need these words:

el elefante	elephant	la pata	foot, paw
el león	lion	la piel	fur
el tigre	tiger	ladrar	to bark
el oso	bear		
el mono	monkey	*Add any other useful words here:*	
la jirafa	giraffe		
el rinoceronte	rhinoceros	....	
el perrito	puppy		
el canario	canary	....	
el conejo de Indias	guinea pig		
el pez de colores	goldfish	....	
la serpiente	snake		
la cola	tail		

Free Time

HOBBIES

◆ **Foundation words**

el tiempo libre	free time	el ciclismo	cycling
el pasatiempo	hobby	el atletismo	athletics
la distracción	hobby, relaxation	el footing	jogging
la afición	interest	el patinaje	skating
principal	main	el patinaje sobre hielo	ice skating
favorito	favourite	el monopatinaje	skateboarding
ser aficionado a	to be a fan of	la natación	swimming
		el esquí acuático	water skiing
jugar a	to play (game)	el windsurf	windsurfing
el juego	game	la vela	sailing
el juguete	toy		
el ajedrez	chess	dar un paseo	to go for a walk
		dar una vuelta	to go for a stroll
leer	to read	patinar	to skate
dibujar	to draw	nadar	to swim
pintar	to paint	montar a caballo	to go riding
ver la televisión	to watch TV	ir de pesca	to go fishing
jugar con el ordenador	to play with the computer	esquiar	to ski
el videojuego	video game	ganar	to win
escuchar la música	to listen to music	perder	to lose
escuchar la radio	to listen to the radio	empatar	to draw
		marcar un gol	to score a goal
		el/la hincha	supporter
tocar	to play (instrument)	el resultado	result
el instrumento	instrument	el partido	match
el piano	piano	el equipo	team
el teclado	keyboard	el campeonato	championship
la guitarra	guitar	el campeón	champion (m)
		la campeona	champion (f)
sacar fotos	to take photos	valer la pena	to be worth it
la máquina de fotos	camera	no vale la pena	it's not worth it
coleccionar	to collect	tener éxito	to be successful
la colección	collection		
		la bolera	bowling alley
los deportes	sports	el polideportivo	sports centre
el fútbol	football	la pista	track
el tenis	tennis	la pista de hielo	ice rink
el baloncesto	basketball	la piscina	swimming pool
el balonvolea	volleyball	el estadio	stadium

la discoteca	disco	la plaza de toros	bull ring
la sala de fiestas	night club	la corrida	bull fight
el teatro	theatre	el torero	bull fighter
la fiesta	party	el toro	bull
el concierto	concert		
el museo	museum	visitar	to visit
el museo de arte	art gallery	salir	to go out
el zoo	zoo	bailar	to dance
el circo	circus	divertirse	to enjoy yourself

◆ **Foundation phrases**

¿Qué haces en tus horas libres?	What do you do in your spare time?
Pues, me gusta leer y patinar.	Well, I like reading and skating.
Juego a cartas.	I play cards.
Juego al futbolín.	I play table football.
Soy miembro del club para jóvenes.	I'm a member of the youth club.
¿Tocas algún instrumento?	Do you play an instrument?
Sí, toco la guitarra.	Yes, I play the guitar.
Me encantan los deportes, sobre todo el fútbol.	I love sports, especially football.
Prefiero escuchar la música.	I prefer to listen to music.
¿Qué tal el partido?	What was the match like?

◆ Higher words

You might also need these words:

interesarse en	to be interested in	la gimnasia	gymnastics
dedicarse a	to go in for	el/la gimnasta	gymnast
entusiasmarse por	to be keen on	dar una caminata	to go hiking
		dar un paseo en barco	to go boating
hacer punto	to knit	remar	to row
coser	to sew	la bicicleta de montaña	mountain bike
la máquina de coser	sewing machine	entrenarse	to train
la costura	sewing	preferir tomar parte	to prefer to take part
el bordado	embroidery		
el encaje	lace	preferir ser espectador	to prefer to be a spectator
coleccionar pegatinas	to collect stickers	el haragán/la haragana del sofá	couch potato
el afiche	poster		
hacer bricolaje	to do DIY	por una parte	on the one hand
		por otra parte	on the other hand
tocar	to play		
el violín	violin		
el violón	double bass	*Add any other useful words here:*

el violonc(h)elo — cello
el clarinete — clarinet
la flauta — flute
la trompeta — trumpet
la batería — drums

los deportes — sports
los dardos — darts
el boxeo — boxing
el béisbol — baseball
el piragüismo — canoeing

....

....

....

....

....

....

◆ Higher phrases

Me gusta relajarme leyendo.	I like to relax with a book.
Los fines de semana suelo ir a la discoteca.	At weekends I usually go to the disco.
Me repugna tener que mirar el boxeo.	I hate having to watch boxing.
Durante las vacaciones lo más importante es pasarlo bien.	During the holidays the most important thing is to have a good time.
¿Cuánto tiempo dura la visita?	How long does the visit last?
Desgraciadamente no tengo bastante dinero.	Unfortunately I don't have enough money.
¡No seas pelma!	Don't be such a bore!

POCKET MONEY

◆ Foundation words

el dinero	money	gastar	to spend
recibir	to get	comprar	to buy
dar	to give	ahorrar	to save
ganar	to earn	invertir	to invest

◆ Foundation phrases

Mi padre me da mil pesetas por semana.	My dad gives me 1,000 pesetas a week.
¿Qué haces con tu dinero?	What do you do with your money?
Con el dinero que recibo compro revistas y discos compactos.	With the money I get I buy magazines and CDs.
Trato de ahorrar un poco también.	I try to save a bit as well.

ARRANGING A MEETING

◆ Foundation phrases

Vamos a la piscina.	Let's go to the swimming pool.
¿Por qué no vamos a...?	Why don't we go to...?
¿Quieres ir...?	Do you want to go...?
¿Dónde nos quedamos?	Where shall we meet?
Nos vemos en el polideportivo.	Let's meet at the sports centre.
¿A qué hora nos vemos?	What time shall we meet?
Tengo ganas de...	I feel like...
¿Qué vamos a hacer?	What shall we do?
Me va muy bien.	That suits me fine.

◆ Higher phrases

Citémonos para las ocho.	Let's meet at eight o'clock.
Citémonos para delante del estadio.	Let's meet in front of the stadium.
Nos vemos mañana en el parque.	See you tomorrow at the park.
¿A qué hora quedamos?	When shall we meet?
¿Estás libre el jueves que viene?	Are you free next Thursday?
¿Cuál prefieres?/¿Cuál te gusta más?	Which do you prefer?
No tengo preferencia.	I have no preference.
¿Te apetece ir al cine?	Do you fancy going to the cinema?
¡En absoluto!	No way!
La idea no apetece.	The idea does not appeal.
¡Buena idea!	Good idea!
¡Ni idea!	I've no idea!
¡De acuerdo!	All right!

Entertainment

TELEVISION AND RADIO

◆ Foundation words

ver	to watch	empezar	to start
el televisor	television	terminar	to finish
el programa	programme	poner	to put on, show
la comedia	comedy		
los deportes	sports	la radio	radio
la emisión deportiva	sports show	en la radio	on the radio
la emisión publicitaria	commercial	escuchar	to listen to
los dibujos animados	cartoons	oír	to listen to, hear
el documental	documentary	la música	music
el drama	drama	la música pop	pop music
el concurso	games show	la música clásica	classical music
las noticias	news	la canción	song
la serie	serial	cantar	to sing
la telenovela	soap opera	el/la cantante	singer
el episodio	episode	el músico	musician (m)
		la música	musician (f)
la lotería	lottery	el concierto	concert
el sorteo	draw	el grupo	group
el premio gordo	jackpot	el conjunto	group
el espectáculo	spectacle	popular	popular

◆ Foundation phrases

¿Puedo escuchar la radio?	Can I listen to the radio?
¿Puedo ver la tele(visión)?	Can I watch TV?
Vi "Neighbours" anoche.	I watched "Neighbours" last night.
Anoche me perdí "Coronation Street".	I missed "Coronation Street" last night.
Vi "Babe" la semana pasada.	I saw "Babe" last week.
En "Only Fools and Horses" David Jason hace el papel de Del Boy.	In "Only Fools and Horses" David Jason plays the part of Del Boy.
No me gustan los anuncios.	I don't like the adverts.
Hoy escuché el concierto de Oasis en la radio.	Today, I listened to an Oasis concert on the radio.
¿Qué piensas de la música clásica?	What do you think of classical music?
¿Qué ponen hoy?	What's on today?
A las ocho hay un concurso que es muy divertido.	At eight o'clock there's a games show which is very funny.
Yo prefiero el fútbol – es más emocionante.	I prefer the football — it's more exciting.
¿Qué tipo de música te gusta?	What sort of music do you like?
Mi cantante favorito es Madonna.	My favourite singer is Madonna.

TVE-1

• JUEVES 7 •

06.15	DULCE ILUSION.
07.00	CHAPULIN COLORADO.
07.30	RING, RING.
09.15	KAINA.
10.00	RUBA.
11.30	NOTICIAS.
11.35	PASA LA VIDA.
14.00	INFORMATIVO TERRITORIAL.
14.30	LA COCINA DE KARLOS ARGUIÑANA.
15.00	TELEDIARIO 1.
15.45	LA DUEÑA.
17.35	SE HA ESCRITO UN CRIMEN.
18.25	AQUI JUGAMOS TODOS.
18.55	NOTICIAS.
19.00	PASA LA VIDA, EDICION DE TARDE.
20.00	INFORMATIVO.
20.20	GENTE.
21.00	TELEDIARIO 2.
21.45	LOTERIA PRIMITIVA.
22.00	HOSTAL ROYAL, MANZANARES.
23.00	LA REVISTA.
01.15	TELEDIARIO 3.
01.45	TENSION EN EL NOCHE.
02.35	HOMBRE RICO, HOMBRE POBRE.
03.25	TELEDIARIO 1.

◆ **Higher words**

You might also need these words:

pasar	to show
el culebrón	soap opera
el serial	soap opera
el telediario	TV news
la emisión	programme
el argumento	plot
el tema	theme
tratar(se) de	to be about
el personaje	character
el/la protagonista	main character
el papel	part, role
hacer el papel de	to play the part of
el papel estelar	star part
ser la estrella	to be the star
tener lugar	to take place
complicado	complicated

Add any other useful words here:

◆ **Higher phrases**

¿De qué se trata?	What is it about?
Mi emisión favorita es un culebrón que tiene lugar en Australia.	My favourite programme is a soap which takes place in Australia.

BOOKS, THEATRE AND THE CINEMA

◆ Foundation words

el teatro	theatre	el cine	cinema
trabajar	to act, perform	el tipo	type, kind
la obra	play	la película	film
el concierto	concert	la comedia	comedy
la sesión	performance	la película de amor	love film
el actor	actor	la película de	adventure film
la actriz	actress	aventuras	
		la película de miedo	horror film
leer	to read	la película de guerra	war film
el periódico	newspaper	la película de	sci-fi film
la revista	magazine	ciencia-ficción	
el tebeo	comic	el dibujo animado	cartoon
el, la cantante	singer	el western	western
el grupo	group		
cantar	singer	fue...	it was...
		aburrido	boring
la taquilla	ticket office	pesado	tedious
la entrada	(entrance) ticket	soso	uninteresting
sacar la entrada	to get, buy a ticket	interesante	interesting
empezar	to start	bueno	good
terminar	to finish	malo	bad
la pantalla	screen	emocionante	exciting
quedar	to be left	regular	average
el asiento	seat	decepcionante	disappointing
hacer cola	to queue up	divertido	amusing
poner	to show a film	triste	sad

◆ Foundation phrases

Leo muchos tebeos.	I read a lot of comics.
¿A qué hora se abre?	What time does it open?
¿A qué hora se cierra?	What time does it shut?
¿Qué ponen en el cine?	What's on at the cinema?
¿Qué tipo de película es?	What sort of film is it?
¿Cuánto cuestan las entradas?	How much do the tickets cost?
¿Quedan entradas?	Are there any tickets left?
¿A qué hora empieza?	What time does it start?
¿A qué hora termina?	What time does it finish?
¿Cuánto dura el concierto?	How long does the concert last?
¿Qué te pareció la película?	What did you think of the film?
En mi opinión el concierto fue muy emocionante.	In my opinion, the concert was very exciting.

7ª **SEMANA** · CINES **RENOIR** PLAZA DE ESPAÑA · CINES **RENOIR** CUATRO CAMINOS

Ganadora de 2 CESARS'95
Mejor director CLAUDE SAUTET . Mejor Actor MICHEL SERRAULT

«El gran espectáculo de la inteligencia...
Cine de gran altura... Una sutil y compleja
historia de amor»
Ángel Fernández-Santos. EL PAIS (★★★★★)
«Precioso y trágico amor tardío»
Carlos Boyero. EL MUNDO (★★★★★)
«Una película hermosa, excelente,
que no hay que dejar de ver»
José Ramón Rey. YA

Premio del Jurado
SEMINCI'95

Premio LOUIS DELLUC '95
Mejor Película Francesa

Premio MELIES'95
Mejor Película del Año

AUTORIZADA PARA TODOS LOS PÚBLICOS

Emmanuelle Béart · Michel Serrault
Jean-Hugues Anglade

NELLY y el Sr. ARNAUD

Una película de Claude Sautet

una coproducción FILMS ALAIN SARDE TF1 FILMS PRODUCTION (Francia) CECCHI GORI GROUP TIGER
CINEMATOGRAFICA (Italia) PROKINO FILMPRODUKTION GMBH (Alemania) con la participación de CANAL+

VERTIGO films

43

◆ Higher words

You might also need these words:

		Add any other useful words here:
estrenarse	to premiere	
la película de espionaje	spy film	....
la película policíaca	detective film	
la película escalofriante	thriller	....
autorizado	suitable for	
recomendado	recommended	....
mayores de	people over (age)	
		....
en versión original	in the original version	
		....
subtitulado	subtitled	
el cinefilo	film fan (m)	....
la cinefila	film fan (f)	
presentar	to put on, show	....

◆ Higher phrases

¿De qué trata ese libro?	What is that book about?
Trata de una mujer a quién le toca la lotería.	It's about a woman who wins the lottery.
La película me hizo mucha gracia.	I found the film very funny.
¿Qué te pareció la obra?	What did you think of the play?
Una película que presenta a Clint Eastwood en el papel de...	A film featuring Clint Eastwood as...

HEADLINES

◆ Higher words

You might need these words:

		Add any other useful words here:
las informaciones	news	
los titulares	headlines	....
pasar, ocurrir	to happen	
acontecer	to happen	....
el acontecimiento	event	
el suceso	event	....

◆ Higher phrases

Según las informaciones de hoy hubo un robo en Londres.	According to today's news there was a robbery in London.
¡Fíjese! ¡Qué horror!	Just imagine! How awful!
Hubo un accidente.	There was an accident.
Hubo un incendio.	There was a fire.

Home Area

HOME ENVIRONMENT

◆ Foundation words

vivir (en)	to live (in)	la polución	contamination
el país	a country	contaminar	to pollute
la región	region	la basura	rubbish
la ciudad	city	el tráfico	traffic
la capital	capital	el embotellamiento	traffic jam
el pueblo	town	el humo	smoke
el mundo	world	ecológico	ccological
la aldea	village		
el barrio	district, area	el campo	country
las afueras	outskirts	el paisaje	countryside
la playa	beach	el bosque	wood
el mar	sea	el árbol	tree
el lugar, el sitio	place	el campo	field
		la hierba	grass
en el campo	in the country	la flor	flower
en la sierra	in the mountains	el pájaro	bird
en la montaña	in the mountains	la granja	farm
a orillas del mar	at the seaside	la cosecha	harvest
en la costa	on the coast	el río	river
en el centro	in the centre	el valle	valley
		el césped	lawn
el medio ambiente	environment	la planta	plant
la industria	industry	cultivar	to grow

◆ Foundation phrases

¿Dónde vives?	Where do you live?
Vivo en un pequeño pueblo industrial.	I live in a small industrial town.
Hay mucha polución.	There's a lot of pollution.
Durham es una ciudad histórica.	Durham is an historical city.
Me gusta mucho el barrio donde vivo.	I like the district where I live very much.
Prefiero la ciudad a los pueblos.	I prefer the city to towns.
No soporto el ruido de los coches.	I can't stand traffic noise.
Me encanta pasear por la montaña.	I love walking in the mountains.
¿Cuánto tiempo hace que vives en Hull?	How long have you lived in Hull?
Hace diez años que vivo aquí.	I've lived here for ten years.
¿Dónde está exactamente?	Where is it exactly?
Está en el norte de Inglaterra.	It's in the north of England.
¿Te gusta vivir en un pueblo?	Do you like living in a town?
¿Qué hay que ver en Newscastle?	What is there to see in Newcastle?
¿Hay mucho que hacer?	Is there a lot to do?

◆ Higher words

You might also need these words:

la población	town, population	la suciedad	dirt, filth
el pueblecito	small town	plantar	to plant
la casita	small house	arrancar	to uproot
la urbanización	housing estate, residential area	destruir	to destroy
		respetar	to respect
la zona	area	mostrar respeto por	to show respect
la zona verde	green belt	recoger	to pick up
los alrededores	outskirts	preocuparse por	to worry about
la vecindad	neighbourhood		
		la naturaleza	nature
costero	coastal	la bahía	bay
pesquero	fishing	el acantilado	cliff
urbano	urban	la foca	seal
urbanizado	built-up	la vertiente	slope
rural	rural	la cumbre	peak, summit
agrícola	agricultural	la roca	rock
campestre	country	la selva	forest
rústico	rustic	la despoblación forestal	deforestation
aldeano	village	el prado	meadow
llano	flat		
montuoso	hilly	*Add any other useful words here:*	
precioso	lovely, charming		
pintoresco	picturesque		
rodeado de	surrounded by	....	
atestado de	packed with		
		....	
estar de bote en bote	to be crowded		
los gases de escape	exhaust fumes	....	
causar daño	to be harmful		
la consecuencia	consequence	....	
crecer	to increase		
el efecto invernadero	greenhouse effect	....	
la contaminación ambiental	environmental pollution	....	
ensuciar	to foul	....	

◆ Higher phrases

Es un pueblecito costero.	It is a small coastal town.
Hay cincuenta mil habitantes.	There are 50,000 inhabitants.
En realidad, no hay mucho que hacer.	There is not really a lot to do.
Las diversiones para los jovenes son muy limitadas.	The entertainment for young people is very limited.

PLACES IN TOWN

◆ Foundation words

el aeropuerto	airport	el museo de arte	art gallery
la estación	railway station	la biblioteca	library
RENFE	Spanish railways	el Ayuntamiento	town hall
la estación de autobuses	bus station	la comisaría	police station
la estación de servicio	service station	el hospital	hospital
el edificio	building	la oficina de turismo	tourist office
el castillo	castle	el centro comercial	shopping centre
la catedral	cathedral	la plaza	square
la iglesia	church	la plaza mayor	main square
el monumento	monument	el puerto	port
el museo	museum	el puente	bridge

◆ Higher words

You might also need these words:

la acera	pavement
el peatón	pedestrian
el paso de peatones	pedestrian crossing
la calle peatonal	pedestrian precinct
la torre	tower
datar de	to date from
el siglo	century
el campanario	church tower
la gasolinera	petrol station
el paseo	boulevard
la fuente	fountain
la abadía	abbey

Add any other useful words here:

....

....

....

....

....

....

....

FESTIVALS

◆ Foundation words

la fiesta	festival	Semana Santa	Holy Week
la costumbre	custom	Viernes Santo	Good Friday
el flamenco	flamenco	Nochebuena	Christmas Eve
el día festivo	holiday	el día de Navidad	Christmas Day
ver	to see	Nochevieja	New Year's Eve
la procesión	procession	el día de Reyes	Twelfth Night, Epiphany

WEATHER

◆ Foundation words

el pronóstico del tiempo	weather forecast	la escarcha	frost
el clima	climate	el trueno	thunder
		el relámpago	lightning
		la nube	cloud
hace...	it is...		
buen tiempo	nice	llover a cántaros	to pour
calor	hot	llueve	it's raining
sol	sunny	nieva	it's snowing
mal tiempo	bad weather	truena	it's thundering
viento	windy	mojarse	to get soaked
frío	cold	mojado	soaked
fresco	cool		
		soleado	sunny
está...	it is...	húmedo	humid, damp
nublado	cloudy, overcast	seco	dry
		caluroso	hot
cubierto	overcast	ventoso	windy
templado	warm, mild	nuboso	cloudy
lloviendo	raining	despejado	cloudless
nevando	snowing	lluvioso	rainy
		nevoso	snowy
hay...	it is...		
niebla	foggy	la temperatura	temperature
neblina	misty	máximo	maximum
hielo	icy	mínimo	minimum
tormenta	stormy	el grado	degree
		bajo cero	below freezing
la tormenta	storm	mejorarse	to improve
la tempestad	storm	soplar	to blow
la borrasca	squall, storm	el viento	wind
la lluvia	rain	la brisa	breeze
el chubasco	shower		
		flojo	light
la inundación	flood	ligero	slight
la nieve	snow	fuerte	strong

◆ Foundation phrases

¿Qué tiempo hace?	What's the weather like?
Hoy hace mucho calor.	It's very hot today.
Mañana va a llover.	It's going to rain tomorrow.
No hace tanto calor aquí.	It's not as hot here.

◆ **Higher words**

You might also need these words:

la estrella	star
la luna	moon
glacial	icy, bitter
el riesgo de	risk of
la amenaza de	threat of
la precipitación	rainfall
la nevada	snowfall
la llovizna	drizzle
el claro	break in clouds
sin nubes	clear (sky)
nubarse	to cloud over
la nubosidad	cloudiness
el descenso	fall
la subida	increase
el mejoramiento	improvement
el empeoramiento	worsening
dar paso a	to give way to

Add any other useful words here:

....

....

....

....

....

....

....

....

 # Nubes y lluvias casi generales

Nuboso salvo en el tercio norte. Chubascos en el sur y sureste y nieve entre los 1.300 a 1.500 metros. Las temperaturas sin cambios salvo Canarias donde descenderán.

GALICIA.—(Máxima:14/Mínima: -1). Nuboso con lluvias débiles. Temperaturas estables.

ASTURIAS, CANTABRIA Y PAIS VASCO.— (Máxima:18/Mínima: 3). Poco nuboso salvo nubes medias y altas. Temperaturas estables.

CASTILLA Y LEON.—(Máxima:15/Mínima: -1). Nuboso con chubascos dispersos. Temperaturas estables.

LA RIOJA, NAVARRA Y ARAGON.— (Máxima:14/Mínima: 0). Nevados en los Pirineos y Sistema Ibérico. Temperaturas estables.

CATALUÑA.—(Máxima:15/Mínima: 4). Nuboso con chubascos en el litoral. Temperaturas diurnas más bajas.

CASTILLA-LA MANCHA Y EXTREMADURA.— (Máxima:15/Mínima: 3). Muy nuboso con nieve sobre los 1.500 metros. Temperaturas estables.

COMUNIDAD VALENCIANA.— (Máxima:16/Mínima: 6). Muy nuboso. Temperaturas estables.

BALEARES.—(Máxima:15/Mínima: 2). Nuboso con lluvias moderadas. Temperaturas estables.

ANDALUCIA.—(Máxima:17/Mínima: 7). Más nuboso en la mitad occidental. Temperaturas estables.

MURCIA.—(Máxima:15/Mínima: 8). Muy nuboso con lluvias. Temperaturas estables.

CANARIAS.—(Máxima:12/Mínima: 14). Nuboso en el norte. Temperaturas bajas.

Shopping

SHOPS

◆ Foundation words

ir de compras	to go shopping	la bodega	wine shop
hacer la compra	to do the shopping	la librería	bookshop
		el quiosco	newspaper stall
abierto	open	el estanco, la tabacalera	tobacconist
cerrado	closed	la farmacia	chemists
		la droguería	drugstore
la tienda	shop	la perfumería	perfume shop
la panadería	bakers	la tienda de confección	clothes shop
la pastelería	cake shop	la zapatería	shoe shop
la confitería	sweet shop	la tienda de discos	record shop
la carnicería	butchers	el videoclub	video shop
la pescadería	fish shop	la tienda de recuerdos	souvenir shop
la frutería	fruit shop	electrodomésticos	electrical goods
la verdulería	greengrocers	los grandes almacenes	department store
la tienda de comestibles	grocers		
el supermercado	supermarket	la peluquería	hairdressers
el mercado	market	la joyería	jewellers
la repostería	cake shop	la relojería	watchmakers

◆ Higher words

You might also need these words:

la lechería	dairy
la charcutería	pork butcher, deli
el hipermercado	hypermarket
la tintorería	dry cleaners
la florería	florists
la ferretería	hardware shop

Add any other useful words here:

....

....

....

....

Información del contenido comercial de nuestra Tienda

7
RESTAURANTE.
CAFETERÍA.
JUGUETES.

6
DEPORTES.
Muebles de
Terraza y Jardín.
Camping.

5
LENCERÍA.
CORSETERÍA.
ZAPATERÍAS.

4
MODA JOVEN.

SHOPPING

◆ Foundation words

la caja	cash desk, till	la venta	sale
la sección	department	la liquidación	sale
la sección de discos	record dept	el precio	price
el probador	changing room	reducido	reduced
el ascensor	lift	a mitad de precio	half-price
la planta baja	ground floor	el descuento	discount
el primer piso	first floor	gratuito, gratis	free
la segunda planta	second floor	empujar	push
tercero	third	tirar	pull
cuarto	fourth	pta	peseta
quinto	fifth	el recibo	receipt
sexto	sixth	la lista	list
		el anuncio	notice
(la) oferta	offer	el surtido	assortment, range
especial	special	la bolsa	bag
(las) rebajas	reductions	envolver	to wrap

◆ Foundation phrases

¿A qué hora se abre?	What time does it open?
¿A qué hora se cierra?	What time does it close?
¿Qué desea?	What would you like?
¿En qué puedo servirle/servirla?	What can I do for you?
Aquí tiene.	Here you are.
¿Algo más?	Anything else?
Nada más gracias.	Nothing else, thank you.
¿Eso es todo?	Is that all?
Sí, eso es todo.	Yes, that is all.
¿Cuánto vale?	How much is it?
¿Cuánto cuesta?	How much does it cost?
Me lo/la quedo.	I'll take it.
Me los/las quedo.	I'll take them.

3 2 I B SS

MODA INFANTIL. Bebés. TEJIDOS Y MERCERÍA.	MODA HOMBRE. AGENCIA DE VIAJES.	MODA MUJER. Peluquería de Señoras.	DISCOS. Librería. Papelería. Prensa y revistas.	SUPERMERCADO.

◆ Higher words

You might also need these words:

deber	to owe	curiosear por	to wander round
la ganga	bargain	las tiendas	the shops
el precio de ocasión	reduced price	curiosear por	to window shop
el precio de saldo	bargain price	los escaparates	
el saldo	sale		
oportunidades	bargains	*Add any other useful words here:*	
últimas novedades	latest fashions		
el carrito	shopping trolley	....	
el mostrador	counter		
el reembolso	refund	....	
el defecto	fault		
gastar	to take a ... shoe	....	
cambiar	to exchange		
devolver	to return	....	
reembolsar	to reimburse		
estar enojado	to be cross	....	
no estar satisfecho	to be dissatisfied		
el servicio a domicilio	home delivery	....	
la fecha de consumo preferente	best before date	....	

QUANTITIES AND MATERIALS

◆ Foundation words

las cantidades	quantities	el oro	gold
el kilo	kilo	la plata	silver
el medio kilo	half kilo	el diamante	diamond
el cuarto de kilo	quarter a kilo	el vidrio	glass
doscientos gramos	200 grammes	el mármol	marble
el tubo	tube	el plástico	plastic
la caja	box	la madera	wood
el paquete	packet	la lana	wool
el bote	pot, jar	la seda	silk
la lata	tin	el algodón	cotton
la botella	bottle	el cuero, la piel	leather
el litro	litre	la pana	corduroy
medio litro	half litre	el nilón	nylon
el par de	pair of	el lino	linen
la docena	dozen	el terciopelo	velvet
el pedazo	piece	de punto	knitted
el trozo	large piece, chunk		

BUYING CLOTHES

◆ Foundation words

la ropa	clothes	los zapatos	shoes
la blusa	blouse	las botas	boots
la camisa	shirt	las zapatillas	trainers
la camiseta	T-shirt	las sandalias	sandals
el pantalón	trousers	la bata de casa	dressing gown
el pantalón corto	shorts		
los vaqueros	jeans	muy	very
el cinturón	belt	demasiado	too
la chaqueta	jacket	grande	big
el traje	suit	pequeño	small
la corbata	tie	mediano	medium (size)
el vestido	dress	largo	large
la falda	skirt	corto	short
el panti/el panty	tights/stockings	barato	cheap
las medias	stockings	caro	expensive
los calcetines	socks	bonito	nice
el jersey	pullover	elegante	smart
la rebeca	cardigan	horrible	awful
el chaleco	waistcoat		
los guantes	gloves	el tamaño, la talla	size (clothes)
el sombrero	hat	el número	size (shoes)
la gorra	cap		
el impermeable	raincoat	las joyas	jewellery
el abrigo	overcoat	el reloj	watch
el paraguas	umbrella	los pendientes	earrings
el chandal	tracksuit	el collar	necklace
los leggings	leggings	la pulsera	bracelet
el leotardo	leotard	la cadena	chain
el bikini	bikini	el anillo	ring
el bañador	trunks	el broche	brooch

◆ Foundation phrases

Quisiera comprar un jersey azul.	I want to buy a blue jumper.
Lo siento, no quedan.	I'm sorry, there are none left.
Me gusta mucho este pantalón.	I like these trousers a lot.
Me lo/la pruebo.	I'll try it on.
Es demasiado grande.	It is too big.
¿Tiene otro en verde?	Have you got another in green?
¿Puedo probármelo?	Can I try it on?
¿No tiene algo más barato?	Haven't you got anything cheaper?
Te va bien.	It suits you.

53

◆ Higher words

You might also need these words:

la cazadora	(bomber) jacket	apretado	tight
la cazadora de piel	leather jacket	de moda	fashionable
la ropa interior	underwear	de molde	perfect, just right
los calzones	boxer shorts	sentar a	to suit
los calconcillos	underpants		
las bragas	knickers	*Add any other useful words here:*	
el sostén	bra		
el pijama	pyjamas	....
el camisón	nightdress		
las alpargatas	canvas sandals	....
estampado	printed	....
liso	plain		
a cuadros	checked	....
a rayas	striped		
con puntos	spotted	....
con manga larga	long sleeved		
con manga corta	short sleeved	....

◆ Higher phrases

Los precios aquí están por las nubes.	The prices here are sky high.
Está pasado de moda.	It's old-fashioned.
El pantalón te sienta bien.	The trousers suit you.
Es una verdadera ganga.	It's a real bargain.
Quiero que me reembolse por favor.	I would like my money back, please.
No estoy satisfecho con estos zapatos.	I'm not satisfied with these shoes.
Gasto el número cuarenta y dos.	I take a size 42 shoe.
¿Cuánto le debo?	How much do I owe you?

SOUVENIRS

◆ Foundation words

los recuerdos	souvenirs	el sombrero	hat
los regalos	presents	la guitarra	guitar
el abanico	fan		
las castañuelas	castanets	el estanco	tobacconist
la cerámica	pottery	el tabaco	tobacco
la muñeca	doll	el puro	cigar
el juguete	toy	los cigarillos	cigarettes
el monedero	purse	las cerillas	matches
el porrón	wine jar	el encendedor	cigarette lighter

ser para	to be for	el maquillaje	make up
es para mí	it is for me	la crema bronceadora	suntan cream
es para mi padre	it is for my dad	el jabón	soap
el periódico	newspaper	la pasta de dientes	toothpaste
la revista	magazine	los tisus	tissues
el tebeo	comic	el desodorante	deodorant
la droguería	drugstore	la colonia	perfume

◆ **Sopa de letras**

Find the words in the wordsearch.

SOMBRERO

CAMISA

BLUSA

FALDA

CORBATA

BOTAS

ZAPATO

CAMISETA

CHAQUETA

PANTALON

VESTIDO

ABRIGO

VAQUEROS

JERSEY

```
S A G I N O L A C N A A
O C Z C A M F R O C T P
S A A A H A O L B E A A
O M P M L A A L U N B B
R O A D I T U Q O O V R
E G A E N S A R T E E I
U I C A A H E A S O S J
Q R P S C R S T T R E J
A B N I B D I A A R O C
V A T M L D P E S R E J
Q O O A O A Y E S R E J
B S F C Z A T A B R O C
```

(Answer on page 96)

55

Public Services

THE POST OFFICE

◆ Foundation words

Correos	post office	a	to
el estanco	tobacconist	Inglaterra	England
la tabacalera	tobacconist	Escocia	Scotland
el buzón	letter box	Irlanda	Ireland
el teléfono	phone	Gales	Wales
querer	to want		
enviar	to send	el sobre	envelope
mandar	to send	el sello	stamp
la carta	letter	dar	to give
la postal	postcard	deme	give me
la tarjeta (postal)	postcard	cerca	nearby

◆ Foundation phrases

Quiero mandar una postal a Inglaterra.	I want to send a postcard to England.
¿Cuánto cuesta?	How much does it cost?
Deme cinco sellos por favor.	Give me five stamps, please.
¿Hay un teléfono cerca de aquí?	Is there a phone near here?
¿Cuál es tu número de teléfono?	What's your phone number?
Compré la postal en el estanco.	I bought the postcard at the tobacconist's.
¿Dónde está el buzón por favor?	Where's the letter box, please?

◆ Higher words

You might also need these words:

en Correos	at the post office
el paquete	parcel
contener	to contain
el contenido	contents
valer	to be worth
el valor	value
el destino	destination
el destinatorio	addressee (m)
la destinatoria	addressee (f)
el/la remitente	sender
echar una carta	to post a letter
la carta urgente	express letter
certificar	to register
certificado	registered
poner un telegrama	to send a telegram
la recogida	collection (mail)

Add any other useful words here:

....

....

....

....

....

....

....

THE BANK

◆ **Foundation words**

en el banco	at the bank	la denominación	denomination
el dinero	money	el coste	cost
el cambio	change		
el cheque	cheque	aceptar	to accept
el billete de banco	bank note	cambiar	to (ex)change
la moneda	coin	valer	to cost
la tarjeta de crédito	credit card	pagar	to pay
el cheque de viajero	traveller's cheque	cambiar	to change
la moneda extranjera	foreign currency	IVA	VAT
la libra (esterlina)	pound (sterling)	incluído	included
el penique	pence, penny	la caja	cash desk, till
la peseta (pta)	peseta	el cajero	cashier (m)
la cantidad	quantity	la cajera	cashier (f)

◆ **Foundation phrases**

¿A cómo está el cambio?	What's the exchange rate?
Quisiera cambiar cincuenta libras en pesetas por favor.	I'd like to change fifty pounds into pesetas please.
¿Me podría dar unas monedas de cien?	Could you give me some 100 peseta coins?
Quiero cobrar un cheque.	I'd like to cash a cheque.
Tenga mi pasaporte.	Here's my passport.
Me da billetes de mil por favor.	Please give me 1,000 peseta notes.
¿Tengo que firmar?	Do I have to sign?
¿A qué hora se abre el banco?	What time does the bank open?
¿A qué ventanilla voy?	Which counter do I have to go to?
¿Cuánto vale la libra esterlina?	What rate is the pound?

LOST PROPERTY

◆ Foundation words

la oficina de objetos perdidos	lost property office	darse cuenta (de que)	to realise that
el monedero	purse	recordar	to remember
la cartera	wallet	lo/la dejé	I left it
la billetera	wallet	los/las dejé	I left them
el bolso	handbag	encontrar	to find
la maleta	suitcase	entregar	to hand in
la cámara fotográfica	camera	devolver	to give back
la marca	make, brand	rellenar	to fill in
		el formulario	form

◆ Foundation phrases

He perdido una maleta negra de cuero.	I have lost a black leather suitcase.
Creo que la dejé en el autobús.	I think I left it on the bus.
En mi cartera había diez mil pesetas.	There was 10,000 pesetas in my wallet.
¿Ha encontrado un reloj de oro, marca Rolex?	Have you found a gold Rolex watch?

THE POLICE

◆ Foundation words

la comisaría	police station	el secuestro	kidnapping
el delito	crime	el secuestrador	kidnapper (m)
el crimen	crime	la secuestradora	kidnapper (f)
la recompensa	reward	el rescate	ransom
recompensar	to reward	el gamberro	hooligan
el ladrón	thief (m)	sospechoso	suspicious
la ladrona	thief (f)	atacar	to attack
robar	to steal	denunciar	to report
el robo	theft, robbery	el atraco	hold-up
cometer	to commit	atracar	to hold up, attack
la pelea	fight	detener	to arrest
pelear	to fight	la cárcel	prison

Getting Around

TRANSPORT

◆ **Foundation words**

el transporte	transport
ir a pie	to go on foot
en autobús	by bus
en coche	by car
en moto	by motorbike
en metro	by underground
en tranvía	by tram
en autocar	by coach
en tren	by train
en barco	by boat
el Talgo, el TER	inter-city high speed train
el rápido	express
el tranvía	stopping train
el ferri	ferry
el taxi	taxi
el camión	lorry
el avión	plane
el viaje	journey
ir	to go
venir	to come
visitar	to visit
la visita	visit
viajar	to travel
el viajero	traveller (m)
la viajera	traveller (f)
el pasajero	passenger (m)
la pasajera	passenger (f)
el billete	ticket
sacar un billete	to buy a ticket
el bonobús	card of 10 tickets
el camionero	lorry driver
el/la taxista	taxi driver
el conductor	driver
el cobrador	conductor
el asiento	seat

libre	free
ocupado	occupied
la taquilla	ticket office
el billete sencillo	single ticket
el billete de ida	single ticket
el billete de ida y vuelta	return ticket
el billete kilométrico	runaround ticket
de primera clase	first class
de segunda clase	standard class
el departamento	compartment
de (no) fumador	(non)smoking
el coche restorán	restaurant car
el coche cama	sleeper
la estación	station
la entrada	entrance
la salida	exit
el andén	platform
la vía	track
la línea	line
la cantina	buffet
la consigna	left luggage
la sala de espera	waiting room
los servicios	toilets
coger	to catch
perder	to miss
transbordarse	to change
hacer transbordo en	to change at
el mozo	porter
el revisor	ticket collector
el horario	timetable
la maleta	suitcase
el anuncio	announcement
atención	(your) attention
procedente de	coming from
con destino a	going to

el retraso	delay	el peligro	danger
el próximo	next	¡ceda el paso!	give way!
		¡curva peligrosa!	dangerous bend
el puerto	port	las obras	roadworks
embarcar	to embark	la velocidad (máxima)	(maximum) speed
desembarcar	to disembark	el desvío	detour
		el peaje	toll
el/la automovilista	motorist	acceso prohibido	no admittance
el/la ciclista	cyclist		
el carnet de conducir	driving licence	el freno	brake
la carretera	main road	el parabrisas	windscreen
la calle	street	el neumático	tyre
la autopista	motorway	el radiador	radiator
el sentido único	one-way street	la batería	battery
el cruce	junction	el motor	engine
el semáforo	traffic lights	el cinturón de	seatbelt
hacer autostop	to hitch-hike	seguridad	
		la gasolina	petrol
conducir	to drive	súper	4-star
arrancar	to start (car)	el aceite	oil
adelantar	to overtake		
aparcar	to park	el aeropuerto	airport
frenar	to brake	el vuelo	flight
		despegar	to take off
el aparcamiento	carpark	aterrizar	to land
la parada de autobuses	bus stop	la azafata	air hostess
la señal	sign	el piloto/la pilota	pilot

INSTRUCCIONES

* Esta tarjeta se utilizará únicamente en las líneas normales de autobuses. Será válida como título de transporte hasta el próximo cambio de tarifas.
* Por favor, no doble Vd. la tarjeta.
* En caso de cualquier anomalía, presente la tarjeta al cobrador del autobús.
* La tarjeta será presentada a cualquier empleado de la empresa que lo solicite.
* Este documento podrá ser retirado en caso de uso indebido.
* 7% I.V.A. Incluido.
* S.O.V. Incluido.
* C.I.F. A-28046316

BONO
BUENO
EL
BONO BUS
• **rapidez**
• **comodidad**
• **economía**

◆ Foundation phrases

¡Buen viaje!	Have a good journey!
Voy al pueblo en autobús.	I go to town by bus.
El viaje dura diez minutos.	The journey lasts 10 minutes.
¿A qué hora llega?	What time does it arrive?
¿A qué hora sale?	What time does it leave?
Un billete de ida y vuelta para Madrid, por favor.	A return ticket to Madrid, please.
¿A qué hora sale el tren?	What time does the train leave?
¿Es éste el autobús para Segovia?	Is this the bus to Segovia?
Quisiera viajar el viernes.	I'd like to travel on Friday.
¿Dónde está la parada?	Where is the bus stop?
Billetes por favor.	Tickets please.
¿Hay un autocar para Barcelona esta tarde?	Is there a coach to Barcelona this afternoon?
¿Qué lugares de interés hay en el pueblo?	What places of interest are there in town?

◆ Higher words

You might also need these words:

el aerodeslizador	hovercraft		la matrícula	number plate
el escúter	scooter		la ventanilla	window
la camioneta	van		la portezuela	door
el ciclomotor	moped		la rueda	wheel
			el volante	steering wheel
el desplazamiento	journey		el faro	headlight
la hora punta	rush hour		el capó	bonnet
el atasco	traffic jam		el maletero	boot
circular	to travel			
desplazarse	to travel		el lavado automático	car wash
detenerse	to stop		comprobar el aceite	to check the oil
estacionar (se)	to park		comprobar la presión	to check the tyres
todos sentidos	all routes		el pinchazo	puncture
la plaza circular	roundabout		la avería	breakdown
preferencia a la derecha	priority from the right		estar averiado	to break down
			arreglar	to mend, fix
			el mecánico	mechanic (m)
el casco	helmet		la mecánica	mechanic (f)
la circulación	traffic		la gasolinera	petrol station
la retención	hold-up		sin plomo	unleaded
el estacionamiento	carpark		el gas-oil	diesel
estacionario	stationary			
el parquímetro	parking meter		¡disminuir velocidad!	reduce speed!
la multa	fine		reducir la velocidad	to reduce speed

tener un accidente	to have an accident	
la colisión	collision	
chocar contra	to bump into	
estrellarse con	to crash into	
a... km por hora	at... km per hour	
frenar en seco	to brake hard	
atropellar	to knock down	
los seguros	insurance	
la ambulancia	ambulance	
quedar totalmente destrozado	to be a write off (car)	
la culpa	blame	
culpar	to blame	
culpable	guilty	

Add any other useful words here:

....

....

....

....

....

....

....

◆ **Higher phrases**

Compruebe el aceite por favor.	Check the oil please.
Mi coche está averiado en la M30.	My car has broken down on the M30.
Podría enviar al mecánico por favor.	Could you send a mechanic, please.
Ha habido un accidente.	There has been an accident.
El coche se saltó el semáforo en rojo.	The car went through the lights on red.
Chocó con un ciclista que sufrió heridas muy graves.	It bumped into a cyclist who suffered serious injuries.
El accidente fue denunciado a la policia.	The accident was reported to the police.

◆ **Rompecabezas**

Fill in the puzzle with the Spanish words for these forms of transport:

1. taxi
2. boat
3. bus
4. plane
5. motorbike
6. bicycle
7. foot
8. train

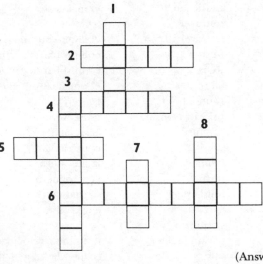

(Answer on page 96)

DIRECTIONS

◆ Foundation words

la oficina de turismo	tourist office	cerca de	near to
informarse	to find out	lejos de	far from
la información	information		
pedir	to ask for	a la izquierda	on the left
el plano	plan	a la derecha	on the right
el folleto	brochure	en la esquina	on the corner
la lista	list		
alquilar	to hire	seguir	to keep on
perdone usted	excuse me	siga todo recto	keep straight on
cerca	near	tuerza a la izquierda	turn left
lejos	far	tuerza a la derecha	turn right
a 5 kilómetros	5 kilometres away	tomar, coger	to take
a 200 metros	200 metres away	la primera calle	the first street
a 2 minutos	2 minutes away	la segunda calle	the second street
		la tercera calle	the third street
delante de	in front of	subir	to go up
detrás de	behind	bajar	to go down
al lado de	next to	doblar la esquina	to turn the corner
enfrente de	opposite	cruzar	to cross
entre	between	el puente	bridge
en el centro de	in the middle of	la plaza	square
al final de	at the end of	la plaza mayor	main square
fuera de	outside	hasta	as far as

◆ Foundation phrases

Perdone señora, ¿por dónde se va a la estación?	Excuse me madam, how do I get to the station?
¿Hay un banco por aquí?	Is there a bank near here?
¿A qué distancia está?	How far is it?
Siga todo recto y está a la izquierda.	Keep straight on and it's on your left.
Tome la segunda calle a la derecha.	Take the second street on the right.
¿Podría indicarme la dirección del banco?	Can you please direct me to the bank?
Me dirijo hacia la playa.	I'm heading for the beach.
Me he extraviado, ¿puede ayudarme?	I'm lost, can you help me?

— NO —
APARCAR

NO SE PASE DE LA RAYA. 🚗🚙

Conduzca con precaución Sobre todo en los adelantamientos
Respete siempre la línea continua Llegará muy lejos

The World of Work

FUTURE PLANS

◆ Foundation words

en el futuro	in the future	ganarse la vida	to earn a living
querer	to want	el servicio militar	military service
pensar	to intend to	hacer la mili	to do military service
esperar	to hope to		
me gustaría	I would like	ganar	to earn
estudiar	to study	pagar bien	to pay well
seguir	to carry on	pagar mal	to pay badly
dejar el colegio	to leave school	el dinero	money
trabajar	to work	tener suerte	to be lucky
buscar	to look for	tener éxito	to be successful
el empleo	job	ir a la universidad	to go to university

◆ Foundation phrases

¿Qué vas a hacer el año que viene?	What are you going to do next year?
El año que viene quiero buscar empleo.	Next year I want to look for a job.
Espero seguir estudiando en el instituto.	I hope to carry on studying at school.
Pienso estudiar las ciencias.	I intend to study science.
Si apruebo mis examenenes quisiera ir a la universidad.	If I pass my exams I'd like to go to university.
Quiero tener éxito en el futuro.	I want to be successful in the future.
Voy a trabajar en una oficina.	I'm going to work in an office.
Me gustaría ser peluquero.	I'd like to be a hairdresser.

◆ Higher words

You might also need these words: *Add any other useful words here:*

tener la intención de	to intend to	....
dedicarse a	to dedicate yourself to	....
hacer el aprendizaje	to serve an apprenticeship	....
el aprendiz	apprentice (m)	....
la aprendiza	apprentice (f)	....
especializarse (en)	to specialise (in)	....
		....
		....

CAREERS

◆ Foundation words

la tienda	shop	el camionero	lorry driver
la oficina	office	la camionera	
el banco	bank	el/la soldado	soldier
la fábrica	factory	el marinero	sailor
la compañía	company	la marinera	
la empresa	firm	el pescador	fisherman
el hospital	hospital	la pescadora	fisherwoman
el garaje	garage	el granjero	farmer
		la granjera	
el empleo	job	el minero	miner
empezar	to start	la minera	
terminar	to finish	el obrero	labourer
trabajar	to work	la obrera	
trabajar de canguro	to babysit	el abogado	lawyer
cuidar	to look after	la abogada	
ganar	to earn	el hombre de negocios	businessman
		la mujer de negocios	businesswoman
interesante	interesting	el vendedor	salesman
aburrido	boring	la vendedora	saleswoman
fácil	easy	el secretario	secretary
difícil	difficult	la secretaria	
duro	hard	el/la recepcionista	receptionist
		el mecanógrafo	typist
ser	to be	la mecanógrafa	
hacerse	to become	el autor	author
quiero ser	I want to be	la autora	
quiero hacerme	I want to become	el actor	actor
		la actriz	actress
el agente, el policía	policeman	el/la artista	artist
la agente, la policía	policewoman	el músico	musician
el bombero	fire-fighter	la música	
la bombera		el fotógrafo	photographer
el cartero	postman	la fotógrafa	
la cartera	postwoman	el ingeniero	engineer
el médico	doctor	la ingeniera	
la médica		el técnico	technician
el enfermero	nurse	la técnica	
la enfermera		el mecánico	mechanic
el/la dentista	dentist	la mecánica	
el/la chófer	chauffeur	el cura	priest
el/la representante	representative	la monja	nun

el panadero	baker	el arquitecto	architect
la panadera		la arquitecta	
el carnicero	butcher	el rey	king
la carnicera		la reina	queen
el farmacéutico	chemist	el príncipe	prince
la farmacéutica		la princesa	princess
el dependiente	shop assistant	el/la jefe	boss
la dependienta		el encargado	person in charge
el camarero	waiter	la encargada	
la camarera	waitress	el marido que trabaja	house-husband
el cocinero	cook	en la casa	
la cocinera		la ama de casa	housewife
el sastre	tailor	el profesor	teacher
la modista	dressmaker	la profesora	
el/la periodista	journalist	estar en paro	to be unemployed

◆ Foundation phrases

Trabajo en una tienda los sábados.	I work in a shop on Saturdays.
Empiezo a las nueve y termino a las cinco.	I start at nine and finish at five o'clock.
Gano quinientas pesetas por hora.	I earn 500 pesetas per hour.
¿En qué trabajan tus padres?	What do your parents do for a living?
Mi madre es arquitecta y mi padre es ingeniero.	My mother is an architect and my father is an engineer.
Mi hermano está en paro.	My brother is unemployed.

VENDEDOR/A

precisa
INGENIERO
(ELECTROTECNIA O SIMILAR)

HOTEL ****
Precisa
COCINERO

Usted puede GANAR
DINERO
Copiando direcciones desde
su casa

SE NECESITAN
AZAFATAS
PARA CAMPAÑA PROMOCIONAL
EN TODA ESPAÑA

SECRETARIA
(SEVILLA)

◆ Higher words

You might also need these words:

el ejército	army	el/la contable	accountant
la marina	navy	el/la oficinista	office worker
la casa	firm	el/la guía de turismo	courier
la agencia de viajes	travel agency	el/la electricista	electrician
en el extranjero	abroad	el fontanero	plumber
		el veterinario	vet
agotador	exhausting	la veterinaria	
estresante	stressful	el cirujano	surgeon
monótono	monotonous	la cirujana	
calificado	skilled	el/la fisioterapeuta	physiotherapist
estimulante	stimulating	el tendero	shopkeeper
estimado	well respected	la tendera	
		el peluquero	hairdresser
la ventaja	advantage	la peluquera	
la desventaja	disadvantage	desempleado	unemployed
		la vacante	vacancy
requerir	to require, need	ofertas	vacancies
conseguir	to get, obtain	demandas	wanted
lograr, ingresar	to start		
despedir	to sack, dismiss		

Add any other useful words here:

la experiencia	experience
la experiencia laboral	work experience
la cualidad	quality
la calificación	qualification
la jornada laboral	work day
el funcionario	civil servant
la funcionaria	

....

....

....

....

◆ Higher phrases

Tengo la intención de hacerme ingeniero.	I intend to become an engineer.
Quisiera trabajar en algo relacionado con las computadoras.	I'd like a job to do with computers.
Me encantaría ser guía de turismo.	I'd love to be a courier.
Hay muchas ventajas – por ejemplo se puede visitar países diferentes.	There are lots of advantages – for example you can visit different countries.
No me apetece trabajar en una ciudad grande.	I don't fancy working in a big city.
Trabajo a tiempo completo/parcial.	I work full/part time.
Estoy sin trabajo./Estoy desempleado.	I'm out of work.
Cobro el desempleo.	I'm drawing unemployment benefit.

◆ Sopa de letras

Find the words in the wordsearch.

REY

CURA

JEFE

ACTOR

SASTRE

CHOFER

MEDICO

AGENTE

PILOTO

CARTERA

TECNICO

CAMARERA

MARINERO

INGENIERA

J	M	M	E	R	O	C	A	M	R	A	M
M	E	D	I	T	O	N	G	E	C	E	A
O	D	F	O	C	A	M	E	D	D	O	R
A	C	L	A	G	R	Y	N	I	C	A	I
P	I	U	E	M	E	H	C	I	A	C	N
P	A	N	R	R	I	O	N	H	M	T	E
A	T	E	M	A	N	C	R	O	A	R	R
E	C	R	E	C	E	A	A	S	R	E	O
C	A	T	O	T	G	M	M	J	E	F	E
I	N	S	R	O	N	A	A	T	R	O	S
C	U	A	A	R	I	R	C	P	A	H	C
S	A	S	M	A	R	E	T	R	A	C	A

(Answer on page 96)

Communications

ADVERTISING

◆ Foundation words

el anuncio	advert	el partido	match
la cartelera	what's on section	el espectáculo	show
	in a newspaper	la fiesta	festival, fete
el informe	announcement	la corrida	bullfight
el póster	poster		
informarse (de)	to find out about	empezar (empieza)	to start (it starts)
pedir	to ask for	cerrar (cierra)	to close (it closes)
la información	information	terminar	to finish
		abrir	to open
el baile	dance	comprar	to buy
el concierto	concert	vender	to sell
la película	film	celebrarse	to take place
el concurso	competition, show	cancelar	to cancel

◆ Foundation phrases

Hay un baile mañana a las ocho de la tarde.	There's a dance tomorrow at eight o'clock.
La película empieza a las diez y termina a las once y media.	The film starts at ten and finishes at half past eleven.
Será un partido muy emocionante.	It will be a very exciting match.
No me quiero perder el espectáculo.	I don't want to miss the show.
Vamos a la fiesta.	Let's go to the festival.
¿Dónde se celebra el concierto?	Where's the concert taking place?
Se celebra en la plaza del mercado.	It's taking place in the market square.

◆ Higher words

You might also need these words:

la exposición	exhibition
la atracción	entertainment
el (día) festivo	holiday
el precio especial	special price
el precio reducido	reduced price
(la) venta de billetes	tickets on sale
gratuito	free
el/la pensionista	pensioner
menores de 18 años	under 18s
mayores de 65 años	over 65s

Add any other useful words here:

....

....

....

....

....

....

THE PHONE

◆ Foundation words

el teléfono	phone	la guía telefónica	phone directory
la cabina	phone box	¡dígame!/¡diga!	hello
telefonear	to phone	soy yo	it's me
llamar	to call	estar comunicando	to be engaged
marcar	to dial	el recado	message
el prefijo	area code	dejar un recado	to leave a message
el número de teléfono	phone number	colgar	to hang up

◆ Foundation phrases

¿Cuál es tu número de teléfono?	What's your phone number?
¡Dígame, soy Jeremy!	Hello, Jeremy speaking.
¿Puedo hablar con Ana?	Can I speak to Ana?
Quisiera dejar un recado.	I'd like to leave a message.
No cuelgue por favor.	Hold the line please.
No contestan.	There's no answer.

◆ Higher words

You might also need these words:

el aparato	handset	el contestador automático	ansaphone
descolgar	to pick up	faxear	to fax
el tono de marcar	dialling tone	el correo electrónico	e-mail
sonar	to ring		
hacer una llamada	to make a call	*Add any other useful words here:*	
a cobro revertido	reversed charges		
la llamada interurbana	long distance call	....	
equivocarse de número	to get the wrong number	....	
el locutorio	phone booth	....	
introducir monedas	to put in coins		
la ranura	slot	....	

◆ Higher phrases

Lo siento, me he confundido de número.	Sorry, I've got the wrong number.
Dile a María que me llame cuando vuelva, por favor.	Tell Maria to call me when she comes back, please.
Quiero hacer la llamada a cobro revertido.	I want to make a reversed charges call.
Te llaman al teléfono.	You're wanted on the phone.
¿Puedes llamarme mañana a las once?	Can you call me tomorrow at eleven?

The Wider World

COUNTRIES

◆ **Foundation words**

el país	country
el mundo	world
extranjero	foreign
Gran Bretaña	Great Britain
Inglaterra	England
inglés/inglesa	English
Escocia	Scotland
escocés/escocesa	Scottish
Irlanda	Ireland
irlandés/irlandesa	Irish
Gales	Wales
galés/galesa	Welsh
España	Spain
español	Spanish
Portugal	Portugal
portugués/portuguesa	Portugese
Andalucía	Andalusia
andaluz/andaluza	Andalusian
Asturias	Asturias
asturiano/asturiana	Asturian
País Vasco	Basque country
vasco	Basque
Castilla	Castile
castellano	Castilian
Cataluña	Catalonia
catalán/catalana	Catalan
Galicia	Galicia
gallego	Galician
Europa	Europe
Austria	Austria
austríaco	Austrian
Bélgica	Belgium
belga	Belgian
Francia	France
francés/francesa	French
Alemania	Germany
alemán/alemana	German
Grecia	Greece
griego	Greek
Holanda	Holland
holandés/holandesa	Dutch
Italia	Italy
italiano	Italian
Rusia	Russia
ruso	Russian
Suecia	Sweden
sueco	Swedish
Suiza	Switzerland
suizo	Swiss
Australia	Australia
australiano	Australian
los Estados Unidos	United States
EE.UU	US
americano	American
La América del Sur	South America
sudamericano	South American
Argentina	Argentina
argentino	Argentinian
Chile	Chile
chileno	Chilean
Méjico, México	Mexico
mejicano, mexicano	Mexican
Perú	Peru
peruano	Peruvian
Venezuela	Venezuela
venezolano	Venezuelan
el Atlántico	Atlantic Ocean
el Mediterráneo	Mediterranean
mediterráneo	Mediterranean
los Pirineos	Pyrenees
los Alpes	Alps

◆ Foundation phrases

¿De qué nacionalidad eres?	What nationality are you?
Soy inglés.	I'm English.
¿De qué parte de España?	From which part of Spain?
Vivo en el noreste de Inglaterra.	I live in the north-east of England.
¿Has visitado España?	Have you been to Spain?
Soy Catalán, pero vivo en Escocia.	I'm Catalan, but I live in Scotland.

◆ Higher words

You might also need these words:

el Reino Unido	United Kingdom	budista	Buddhist
Cornualles	Cornwall	árabe	Arabic
el País de los Lagos	Lake District	africano	African
londinense	(of) London	europeo	European
madrileño	of Madrid	escandinavo	Scandinavian
sevillano	Sevillian		
cordobés/cordobesa	of Cordoba	*Add any other useful words here:*	
el Canal de la Mancha	English Channel		
el túnel del Canal de la Mancha	Channel Tunnel	....	
las (Islas) Baleares	Balearic Islands	....	
las (Islas) Canarias	Canary Islands		
Turquía	Turkey	....	
Túnez	Tunisia		
		....	
cristiano	Christian		
católico	Catholic	....	
judío	Jewish		
protestante	Protestant	....	
musulmán/musulmana	Moslem		
hindú	Hindu	....	

POINTS OF THE COMPASS

◆ Foundation words

ser de	to come from	el noreste	north-east
el norte	north	el nordeste	north-east
el sur	south	el noroeste	north-west
el este	east	el sudeste	south-east
el oeste	west	el suroeste	south-west

ENVIRONMENTAL AND WORLD ISSUES

◆ Higher words

You might also need these words:

interesarse en	to be interested in	la actitud	attitude
preocuparse	to be concerned	humanitario	humanitarian
la ecología	ecology	el Tercer Mundo	Third World
el/la ecologista	conservationist	la hambre	famine
el ecologismo	conservation	morir de hambre	to starve
los temas verdes	green issues	la sequía	drought
el Partido Verde	Green Party	luchar por	to fight for
la naturaleza	nature	la independencia	independence
la especie en peligro	endangered	el desarrollo	development
(de extinción)	species	económico	economic
maltratar	to ill-treat	la paz	peace
proteger	to protect		
la protección	protection	los problemas sociales	social problems
el proyecto	project	el paro	unemployment
esforzarse a	to make an effort to	la violencia	violence
el esfuerzo	effort	el divorcio	divorce
solucionar	to solve	la droga	drugs
poner en libertad	to set free	el robo	theft
destruir	to destroy	la huelga	strike
la capa de ozono	ozone layer	la manifestación	demonstration
el efecto invernadero	greenhouse effect		
los seres humanos	human beings	*Add any other useful words here:*	
la humanidad	mankind		
		....	
el gobierno	government		
el político	politician (m)	....	
la política	politician (f)		
colaborar	to collaborate	....	

◆ Higher phrases

Me interesan mucho los asuntos ecológicos.
I'm very interested in environmental issues.

Creo que la contaminación es un problema mundial.
I think that pollution is a world-wide problem.

Me preocupo mucho por las especies en peligro.
I'm very concerned about endangered species.

Es preciso que todos los países colaboren más para solucionar el problema del agujero en la capa del ozono.
It's necessary for all countries to collaborate more to solve the problem of the hole in the ozone layer.

Tourism

HOLIDAYS

◆ Foundation words

el turismo	tourism	descansar	to rest
las vacaciones	holidays	pasearse	to go for a walk
las vacaciones ...		sacar fotos	to take photos
de verano	summer holiday	comprar	to buy
de invierno	winter holiday	el regalo	present
de primavera	spring holiday	el recuerdo	souvenir
de otoño	autumn holiday	jugar	to play
de Navidad	Christmas holiday	practicar	to do, go
veranear	to spend the summer	el windsurf	windsurfing
pasar	to spend	la vela	sailing
una semana	a week	esquiar	to ski
quince días	fortnight		
un mes	a month	ir	to go
		visitar	to visit
en	at, in	ver	to see
el campo	country	el castillo	castle
la montaña	mountain	el monumento	monument
la sierra	mountain range	el sitio, el lugar	place
el lago	lake		
el pueblo	town	el ambiente	atmosphere
la ciudad	city	histórico	historical
la playa	beach	turístico	tourist
el mar	sea	típico	typical
la ola	wave	interesante	interesting
la arena	sand	aburrido	boring
		bonito	nice
el apartamento	apartment	feo	ugly, awful
la caravana	caravan	tranquilo	peaceful
el cámping	campsite	ruidoso	noisy
el hotel	hotel		
en el extranjero	abroad	me gusta ...	I like ...
		preferir	to prefer
estar de vacaciones	to be on holiday	valer la pena	to be worth it
ir de vacaciones	to go on holiday	recomendar	to recommend
hacer cámping	to go camping	la gente	people
tomar el sol	to sunbathe	el/la turista	tourist
bañarse	to bathe	el/la guía	guide
nadar	to swim	el/la veraneante	holiday maker
divertirse	to enjoy yourself		
pasarlo bien	to have a good time		

To describe holiday weather, see page 48.

◆ Foundation phrases

Hay mucho que hacer.	There is a lot to do.
Había mucho/poco que hacer.	There was a lot/not much to do.
Hago una excursión.	I'm going on a trip.
¿Qué haces normalmente durante las vacaciones?	What do you normally do during the holidays?
Por lo general voy de vacaciones con mis padres.	I usually go on holiday with my parents.
Solemos ir a la Costa del Sol para dos semanas.	We usually go to the Costa del Sol for two weeks.
Tomo el sol y practico el windsurf.	I sunbathe and go windsurfing.
El año pasado fui a Francia.	Last year I went to France.
Viajé en coche con mis amigos.	I travelled by car with my friends.
Nos quedamos en un cámping.	We stayed at a campsite.
Vi muchas cosas interesantes.	I saw lots of interesting things.
Hizo mucho calor y lo pasé muy bien.	It was very hot and I had a great time.

◆ Higher words

You might also need these words:

el intercambio	exchange
el veraneo	summer holiday
el lugar de veraneo	summer resort
el par de semanas	couple of weeks
la quincena	fortnight
la temporada alta	high season
de temporada baja	off-peak
explorar	to explore
disfrutar de	to enjoy
tumbarse al sol	to sunbathe
broncearse	to get a suntan
la simpatía	friendliness
la gastronomía	good food
la excursión de un día	day trip
la caseta	bathing hut
la plancha, la tabla	surf board
el/la tablista	windsurfer
beneficiarse de	to benefit from
crecer	to grow
generar	to generate
contribuir a	to contribute to
ofrecer	to offer
el desarrollo económico	economic development
la industria del turismo	tourist industry

Add any other useful words here:

....

....

....

....

....

....

....

....

◆ Higher phrases

Este año voy a visitar a mi correspondiente española.	I'm going to visit my Spanish penfriend this year.
Pasaremos una semana en su piso en Barcelona, y una semana en la costa.	We'll spend one week in her flat in Barcelona and one week on the coast.
En realidad prefiero veranear a orillas del mar.	In fact, I prefer to spend the summer holidays at the seaside.
Siempre hay un montón de cosas que hacer.	There's always loads of things to do.
¿Puede informarme sobre las excursiones a Segovia por favor?	Can you give me some information about the trips to Segovia, please?

HOTELS

◆ Foundation words

el hotel	hotel	la comida	lunch
la habitación con una cama (dos camas)	single room (double)	la cena	evening meal
		quedarse	to stay
la habitación individual	single room	para una noche	for one night
la habitación doble	double room	a partir de	from (date)
libre	free		
con baño	with a bath	la recepción	reception
la ducha	shower	el/la recepcionista	receptionist
el lavabo	washbasin	la llave	key
el wáter	toilet	el número	number
el balcón	balcony	la reserva	reservation
la terraza	terrace	reservar	to reserve
la vista	view	firmar	to sign
la piscina	swimming pool	el pasaporte	passport
el ascensor	lift	el nombre	name
		el apellido	surname
media pensión	half-board	rellenar	to fill in
pensión completa	full-board	el formulario	form
el desayuno	breakfast	pagar	to pay

◆ Foundation phrases

¿Tiene una habitación con ducha?	Have you got a room with a shower?
Quiero pensión completa por favor.	I'd like full-board, please.
Es para dos noches.	It's for two nights.
¿Hay un restaurante en el hotel?	Is there a restaurant in the hotel?
¿A qué hora se sirve el desayuno?	What time is breakfast served?
No hay papel higiénico.	There's no toilet paper.
No funciona la ducha/la luz.	The shower/light doesn't work.

HOTEL LAS VEGAS

34 habitaciones nuevas con aire acondicionado, a pie de playa, caja fuerte, doble acristalamiento, totalmente insonorizadas, TV satélite, secadores de pelo en baño de marmol, terraza y vista al mar.

◆ Higher words

You might also need these words:

la casa de huéspedes	guest house
el precio máximo	maximum price
el depósito	deposit
disponible	available
camas gemelas	twin beds
el personal	staff
el hotelero/la hotelera	hotel keeper
el director/la directora	manager
el huésped	guest
disfrutar	to make use of
disponer de	to have at your disposal
la piscina cubierta	indoor pool
la piscina climatizada	heated pool
amplio	spacious
el cargo	charge
cargar	to charge
la factura	bill
quejarse	to complain
enojarse	to get angry
enfadarse	to be annoyed
decepcionado	disappointed

Add any other useful words here:

....

....

....

....

....

....

....

....

....

....

◆ Higher phrases

Quisiera reservar una habitación doble con baño y una habitación individual con ducha para una semana, del 20 al 27 de julio.

Le ruego me mande una tarifa de precios.

I'd like to reserve a double room with a bath and a single room with a shower for one week, from 20 to 27 July.

Could you send me a price list.

CAMPING

◆ Foundation words

el cámping	campsite	el restaurante	restaurant
acampar	to camp	el bar	bar
hacer cámping	to go camping	la cafetería	café
el/la campista	camper	los servicios	toilets
la tienda	tent	las duchas	showers
la caravana	caravan	el agua potable	drinking water
el adulto	adult		
el niño/la niña	child	el colchón de aire	airbed
		el saco de dormir	sleeping bag
preferir	to prefer	la lámpara de bolsillo	torch
(en) la sombra	(in) the shade	la pila	battery
el árbol	tree	las cerillas	matches
las facilidades	facilities	el abrelatas	tin opener
la lavandería	laundry	el sacacorchos	corkscrew
el parque infantil	children's play area	encender un fuego	to light a fire

◆ Foundation phrases

¿Hay sitio en el cámping?	Have you got any room on the campsite?
¿Cuánto cuesta por noche/por persona?	How much does it cost per night/person?
Somos cuatro: dos adultos y dos niños.	There are four of us: two adults and two children.
Prefiero estar en la sombra.	I prefer to be in the shade.

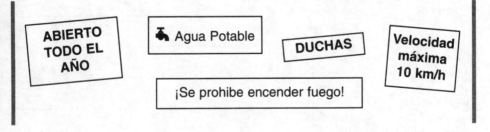

◆ Higher words

You might also need these words:

montar una tienda	to put up a tent	el cubo de basura	dustbin
la parcela	pitch	la papelera	litter bin
la dirección	management	la botella de gas	gas cylinder
el personal	personnel	el hornillo de gas	camping stove
vigilado	supervised	la barbacoa	barbecue
equipado	equipped	el enchufe	electric socket
los aseos	toilets	la norma	rule

la regla	rule
el reglamento	regulations
cumplir	to comply with
respetar	to respect
rogar	to request
recordar	to remind
prohibir	to prohibit
prohibido	prohibited
el permiso	permission
pedir permiso	to ask permission
guardar silencio	to keep quiet

Add any other useful words here:

....

....

....

....

....

◆ Higher phrases

Puede reservarme un espacio para dos días en su cámping.	Could you reserve me a place for two days on your campsite.
Hay que respetar el reglamento.	You have to respect the rules.
Está estrictamente prohibido cambiar de emplazamiento sin permiso.	It is strictly prohibited to change site without permission.
Se prohibe encender fuego.	You are not allowed to light fires.

CAMPING MUNICIPAL DE CINTRUENIGO

CINTRUENIGO

TEL. (948) 81 24 77

■ SITUACION

La villa de Cintruénigo cuenta con más de 5.000 habitantes y ofrece al turista todos los servicios para hacer más cómoda su estancia. El cámping se encuentra situado a 200 m. del núcleo urbano. Acceso: N-113 Soria-Pamplona. Comarcal N-160 Tudela-Fitero, à 18 Kms. de Tudela, capital de la Ribera.

Capacidad: 200 Plazas.   Categoria: 2ª

OTHER ACCOMMODATION

◆ Foundation words

el albergue juvenil	youth hostel	la sábana	sheet
el dormitorio	dormitory	el jabón	soap
el comedor	dining room	la comida	meal
la cocina	kitchen	la pensión	boarding house
el salón	lounge	el chalet	villa, cottage
alquilar	to hire	la granja	farmhouse

◆ Higher words

You might also need these words:

la tarjeta de miembro	membership card
la vivienda	apartment
el estudio	studio flat
espacioso	spacious
todo confort	all mod cons
en buenas condiciones	in a good state
de reciente construcción	recently built

Add any other useful words here:

....

....

....

....

LIFE ABROAD

◆ Higher words

You might need these words:

saludar	to greet	rebozar	to fry in batter
estrecharse la mano	to shake hands	el pudin	pudding
besarse	to kiss each other	el curry	curry
la siesta	nap	las pastas	pasta
tomar una siesta	to have a siesta	la paella	paella
		la tortilla española	Spanish omelette
el paseo	stroll in street	la tortilla de patatas	Spanish omelette
pasearse	to stroll around meeting friends	el pollo al ajillo	chicken cooked in garlic
la juerga	a good night out	la fabada	stew of broad beans, pork, etc.
ir de juerga	to go out for a good time	el cochinillo	suckling pig
tomar una copa	to have a drink		

Add any other useful words here:

el rosbif	roast beef
asar	to roast
pescado frito con patatas fritas	fish and chips

....

....

◆ **Crucigrama: en el hotel**

1 ¿Dónde está la **X**? Quiero nadar.
2 Quiero una habitación **X**.
3 No hay baño pero hay una **X**.
4 ¿Cómo me voy a lavar? No hay **X**.
5 ¿A qué hora se sirve el **X**?

6 Es fácil subir a la habitación en el **X**.
7 Trabaja en la recepción.
8 El camarero trabaja en el **X** del hotel.
9 ¿Quiere **X** completa?
10 ¿Cuánto cuesta por **X**?
11 Necesitas una **X** para entrar en la habitación.

(Answer on page 96)

81

Building up Vocabulary

It is surprising how quickly you can build up vocabulary.
Try to make learning an enjoyable process:

- set yourself realistic targets
- get a friend to test you
- make learning cards
- use a computer
- if you like drawing, do some illustrations.

The following pages have suggestions to help you increase your vocabulary.

 A lot of words are the same in Spanish as they are in English:

Examples: el hotel   el hospital   el animal   el póster   el hámster

Make your own list here:

....

....

....

....

Many words in Spanish are very similar to their English equivalent. The following examples should help you to work out their meaning.

2 **Sometimes the Spanish word simply adds another letter to the English:**

Examples: el plano   el monumento   la visita   la lista   el uniforme   el restaurante

Make your own list here:

....

....

....

....

3 Spanish words ending in "sión" are often the same,
or nearly the same, as English word ending in "sion":

Examples: excursión (excursion)   decisión (decision)   discusión (discussion)

Make your own list here: ....

....

....

....

....

4 Words ending in "tion" in English are often
changed to "ción" in Spanish:

Examples: nación (nation)   información (information)   estación (station)

Make your own list here: ....

....

....

....

....

5 "ph" in English is replaced in
Spanish by the letter "f":

Examples: elefante (elephant)   foto (photo)   farmacia (pharmacy)   física (physics)

Make your own list here: ....

....

....

....

....

6 Words ending in "y" in English often change to "ía" or "ia" in Spanish:

Examples: biología (biology)   tecnología (technology)   categoría (category)

Make your own list here:

....

....

....

....

7 The ending "ty" in English often becomes "dad" in Spanish:

Examples: la ciudad (city)   la electricidad (electricity)   la calidad (quality)

Make your own list here:

....

....

....

....

8 "ic(al)" in English is often translated by "ico" in Spanish:

Examples: eléctrico (electric[al])   práctico (practical)   físico (physical)

Make your own list here:

....

....

....

....

**"th" in English often becomes
simply "t" in Spanish:**

Examples: catedral (cathedral)   teatro (theatre)   simpatía (sympathy)

Make your own list here:

....

....

....

....

10 **Words ending in "ant" or "ent" in English often
become "ante" or "ente" in Spanish:**

Examples: protestante (protestant)   incompetente (incompetent)   elefante (elephant)

Make your own list here:

....

....

....

....

11 **Adverbs ending in "ly" end
in "mente" in Spanish:**

Examples: normalmente (normally)   generalmente (generally)

Make your own list here:

....

....

....

....

The prefix "un" usually becomes "in" in Spanish:

Examples: incompleto (unfinished)   injusto (unfair)   insoportable (unbearable)

Make your own list here:

....

....

....

....

....

13 **Verbs in Spanish are very often based upon a noun:**

Examples: la cena/cenar (supper/to have supper)   el juego/jugar (game/to play)

Make your own list here:

....

....

....

....

....

14 **Some adjectives (describing words) are often similar to the noun:**

Examples: la religión/religioso (religion/religious)   el ruido/ruidoso (noise/noisy)

Make your own list here:

....

....

....

....

....

The Spanish endings "ito/a" and "illo/a" are used to make something smaller:

Examples: la casa/la casita (house/small house)   el perro/el perrito (dog/puppy)

Make your own list here:

....

....

....

....

....

16 **The Spanish ending "ón/ona" is used to make something bigger:**

Example: el hombre/el hombrón (man/big man)

Make your own list here:

....

....

....

....

....

If you come across a word you have never seen before, try to guess its meaning by looking for clues. Ask yourself:

■ Is it like the English?

Examples:

el estómago	stomach
la ambulancia	ambulance

■ Can you see part of a word you already know within the word?

Examples:

insolación
you know the word "sol" means "sun" and, from the rest of the sentence, you may work out that "insolación" means "sunstroke"
acercarse
you know the word "cerca" means "near" – this is a verb which means "to come near", "to approach"

■ Is the word similar to a word you may have learned in French?

Examples:

iglesia	(like église)	church
piscina	(like piscine)	swimming pool
grande	(like grand)	big

■ Is the word made up of two parts?

Examples:

el lavaplatos	dishwasher
el sacacorchos	corkscrew
el abrelatas	tin opener

Words to Watch Out For

 1 **Sometimes words can be confusing if there is only one letter different:**

Examples:

hoy	today	el jamón	ham
hay	there is/are	el jabón	soap
el hombre	man		
la hambre	hunger	casado	married
		cansado	tired
el puerto	port		
la puerta	door	la playa	beach
		la plaza	square
el cuarto	room		
cuatro	four	caro	expensive
		la cara	face
¿cuándo?	when		
¿cuánto?	how much	el bote	can
		la bota	boot
pero	but		
el perro	dog	libre	free
		la libra	pound
lleno	full		
llano	flat	el plato	plate
		la plata	silver
llegar	to arrive		
llevar	to wear, carry	gastar	to spend
llenar	to fill	ganar	to earn, win

 2 **Sometimes the accent makes all the difference:**

Examples:

si	if
sí	yes
sólo	only
solo	alone

Sometimes the way the letters are
arranged can lead to confusion:

Examples:

el camino   road
el camión   lorry

la película   film
la peluquería   hairdressers

la ciudad   city
cuidado   be careful

 Amigos falsos (false friends). Sometimes a Spanish word looks
like a word in English, but means something completely different:

Examples:

el pan	bread	suspender	to fail (exam)
la ropa	clothes	asistir	to attend
largo	long	el conductor	driver
el motor	engine	los parientes	relatives
el músico	musician	la mermelada	jam
el fotógrafo	photographer	la planta baja	ground floor
embarazada	pregnant	el gato	cat
la librería	bookshop	mayor	elder, main
el wáter	toilet	la sopa	soup
el pie	foot	estar constipado	to have a cold
el éxito	success		

 Sometimes a word has more than
one meaning in Spanish:

Examples:

la muñeca	wrist	doll
la tienda	shop	tent
la piel	skin	leather
llevar	to wear	to carry
la fiesta	festival	party
el campo	field	country
duro	hard	
el duro	5 peseta coin	

Writing Tips

For the foundation writing paper at GCSE you will be asked to write a list or message and a letter, which is usually of an informal nature to a friend, but which could be of a formal nature to a hotel, campsite, etc. Here are some tips for you:

■ Keep your writing simple. Use words and phrases in Spanish that you have used before and which you feel confident about.

■ NEVER write out your answer in English before trying to translate it into Spanish – that can lead to all sorts of mistakes.

■ In the exam you will be allowed to use a dictionary, but be very careful to make sure you find the right word.

■ MAKE SURE YOU COVER ALL THE POINTS YOU ARE ASKED TO. This is most important because, if you don't, you will lose marks on content. Put a tick next to each task on the question paper once you have answered it.

■ Sometimes you can get clues from the letter on the question paper – it is simply a question of re-using some of the words and phrases for your own purposes. Remember in your reply that you are talking about yourself, so in the present tense you need to change regular verb endings to "o":

Examples:

¿Por qué quieres este empleo?	Why do you want this job?
Quiero este empleo porque...	I want this job because...
¿Adónde vas de vacaciones?	Where are you going on holiday?
Voy a España,	I'm going to Spain.

■ In the letter you will also have to ask some questions. If it is a letter to a friend, remember that the verb will probably end in "s":

Examples:

¿Adónde vas?	Where are you going?
¿Tienes...?	Have you got ...?
¿Prefieres...?	Do you prefer...?
But	
¿Te gusta el colegio?	Do you like school?
¿Te gustan los deportes?	Do you like sports?

■ If the letter is formal and you are asking questions, remember to remove the "s" from the end of the verb.

Example:

¿Puede reservarme...?	Can you reserve me...?

- Here are some useful questions for letters:

¿Qué tiempo hace...?	What is the weather like...?
¿Hay...?	Is/are there...?
¿A qué hora...?	What time...?
¿Cómo es...?	What is... like?
¿Cual es/qué es...?	What is...?
But	
¿Cómo se llama...?	What is... called?
¿Cómo se llama tu hermano?	What is your brother called?
¿Por qué...?	Why...?
¿Cuánto tiempo...?	How long...?

- Remember to put your town and date on the right of your letter.

Example:

Durham, 21 de mayo

- Make sure you have the correct beginning for your letter.

Examples:

Querido	(to a male friend)
Querida	(to a female friend)
Muy señor mío	(to a male stranger)
Muy señora mía	(to a female stranger)

- Make sure you have the correct ending for your letter.

Examples:

un abrazo de	(to a friend)
hasta pronto	(to a friend)
con el afectuoso saludo	(to a friend)
le saluda atentamente	(to a stranger)

- Take care in your work. Try to be neat and accurate. Avoid crossing out. If you have time, do a rough version, then copy it up. If one sentence is causing you problems, write it out in rough on the supplementary paper provided.

- Check for:

a) Spellings – remember that the only double consonants in Spanish are "ll" "cc" "rr" "nn"

b) Agreement of describing words – "la ciudad bonita"

c) Position of describing words – in Spanish, most come after the noun: "la falda azul"

d) Verbs – make sure that it is the right verb and that you have: the right tense, the right person and the right ending

e) "a" followed by "el" changing to "al" – "fui al pueblo"

f) "de" followed by "el" changing to "del" – "saqué la foto del monumento"

- Try to use separate paragraphs for the different points you are making. This is quite easy if you look back to the letter on the question paper.

- Don't be afraid to show off a bit to the examiner if there are things you have learned which you feel you can bring into your reply. The examiner will be impressed by such things as:

a) "al" "antes de" "después de" "para," "sin" + infinitive
b) Opinions – "me gusta" etc.
c) Linking words – "cuando" "donde" "que" "porque"
d) Expressions using "qué" – "qué bién"
e) "Tener" expressions – "tengo que..." (I've got to...)
f) Idioms – "lo pasé estupendamente"
g) If you can use different tenses:

juego	I play
voy a jugar	I'm going to play
jugaré	I will play
jugué	I played
me gustaría...	I would like...

H I G H E R   L E V E L

At this level you will be required to write a letter (formal or informal) in which you will be asked to write about past, present and future events and to express personal opinions. You will also be asked to write a text which demonstrates your ability to write descriptively or imaginatively, for example, an article, account, letter, publicity material.

- Obviously, a lot of what was said for Foundation Tier still applies here. Do make sure you cover all the points and check for mistakes.

- At this level, the examiner will be looking for a good command of tenses, so as well as the present, preterite and immediate future, you must know the future, perfect and imperfect really well.

- The following constructions are worth learning:

estar a punto de	to be on the point of
estar para	to be about to
volver a	to do something again
tardar en	to take so long doing something
mientras + imperfect	while someone was doing something
ojalá (+ subjunctive)	if only
lo (+ adjective):	
lo importante	the most important thing

93

- Bring in some of the following for which you will be given credit:

primero	first	aunque	although
en primer lugar	firstly	apenas	hardly, scarcely
para empezar	to start with	en lugar de	instead of
por fin	finally	además de	as well as
finalmente	eventually	a pesar de	in spite of
por una parte	on the one hand	a causa de	because of
por otra parte	on the other hand	en cuanto a	with regard to
por lo visto	evidently	tal vez, acaso	perhaps
según parece	apparently	a lo mejor	probably, maybe
de todas formas	anyway	sin duda	no doubt
en efecto	indeed	o sea	that is to say
en realidad	in fact	así que	anyway
según	according to		

- The following impersonal verbs are useful:

me interesa	I'm interested in
me interesaría	I would be interested in
encantar	to love
entusiasmar	to be keen on
apetecer	to fancy
hacer falta	to need
gustar	to like

- At this level you need to expand as much as possible, so join sentences together with words like "que" "cuando" "donde" "porque". A good way to expand your work is to ask yourself a series of questions: what? when? why? where? how? etc.

- Try to bring in opinions:

en mi opinión	in my opinion
me parece que	I think that
quisiera	I should like
espero que	I hope that
estar a favor de	to be in favour of
estar en contra de	to be against
me opongo totalmente a	I'm totally opposed to
me pregunto si	I wonder if
me sorprende que	I'm surprised that
(no) estoy de acuerdo	I (don't) agree
yo creo que	I think that
lo siento mucho pero	I'm very sorry but
me hace mucha ilusión	I'm looking forward to
tu carta me hizo mucha ilusión	I was thrilled to get your letter
¿qué opinas de...?	what's your opinion of...?

Dictionary Skills

You will be allowed access to bilingual dictionaries throughout the whole of the Reading and Writing tests. You will also be allowed to use a dictionary and make notes during the preparation time for the Speaking tests, but you will not be allowed to take the dictionary into the exam. In Listening, you will be given five minutes reading time at the start of the tests and five minutes checking time at the end, during which time you will be allowed to use a dictionary.

- Dictionaries cannot replace a broad-based vocabulary of which you have a good working knowledge – they should really be seen as a tool to supplement what you already know and, consequently, should be used sparingly.

- Dictionary skills are acquired with practice, so you should start to develop them at an early stage in your course. It's no good relying on a dictionary in the exam if you have never used one before.

- If you have looked up a word in English and found what you think is the right Spanish word, check it in the Spanish-English part of the dictionary. The same applies when looking up a Spanish word (i.e. check it in the English section).

- In the exam, time is precious, so make a list of the words you really don't know. This list should be kept to a minimum.

- It is important that when you look up a word you know what sort of word it is. In the dictionary this is indicated before the word itself (usually abbreviated):

n	noun
vt or vi	verb
adj	adjective
adv	adverb
prep	preposition

- Remember that if you are looking up a word in Spanish, "ll" and "ch" are letters in their own right and have a place of their own in the dictionary;
  "ch" comes after the section of words starting with "c"
  "ll" comes after the section of words starting with "l"

Answers

◆ **Ejercicio** page 16

1. ciencias	2. dibujo	3. inglés	4. cocina
5. historia	6. alemán	7. música	8. religión

◆ **Sopa de letras** page 55

```
S A G I N O L A C N A A
O C Z C A M F R O C T P
S A A A H A O L B E A A
O M P M L A A L U N B B
R O A D I T U Q O O V R
E G A E N S A R T E E I
U I C A A H E A S O S J
Q R P S C R S T T R E J
A B N I B D I A A R O C
V A T M L D P E S R E J
Q O O A O A Y E S R E J
B S F C Z A T A B R O C
```

◆ **Rompecabezas** page 62

1. taxi	2. barco	3. autobús	4. avión
5. moto	6. bicicleta	7. pie	8. tren

◆ **Sopa de letras** page 68

```
J M M E R O C A M R A M
M E D I T O N G E C E A
O D F O C A M E D D O R
A C L A G R Y N I C A I
P I U E M E H C I A C N
P A N R R I O N H M T E
A T E M A N C R O A R R
E C R E C E A A S R E O
C A T O T G M M J E F E
I N S R O N A A T R O S
C U A A R I R C P A H C
S A S M A R E T R A C A
```

◆ **Crucigrama: en el hotel** page 81

1. piscina	2. individual	3. ducha	4. jabón
5. desayuno	6. ascensor	7. recepcionista	8. comedor
9. pensión	10. persona	11. llave	